THE SOUNDS AND SMELLS OF MY CHILDHOOD

Growing Up in the Soo's East End in the 1950s

PART II

MIKE MCCARTHY

Scriptor House LLC

2810 N Church St Wilmington, Delaware, 19802

www.scriptorhouse.com

Phone: +1302-205-2043

Published by Scriptor House LLC

Paperback ISBN: 979-8-88692-229-5

eBook ISBN: 979-8-88692-230-1

Hardback ISBN: 979-8-88692-310-0

Contents

The Smells of My Childhood

My St. Mary's River

I long for the dear old river,

Where I dreamed my youth away,

For a dreamer lives forever,

And a toiler dies in a day.

So dream your dreams, Then write them,

But you have to live them first.

(John T. McCarthy, "In My Father's Own Words")

Foreword

When Mike McCarthy contacted me to write the foreword for *The Sounds and Smells of My Childhood*, I had no idea that the project would generate such a groundswell of support and enthusiasm in the Soo Theatre, a vital part of our art community in Sault Sainte Marie, Michigan. It has been a pleasure to witness the good that has come from one person's determination to make a difference for his hometown.

It's no secret that small towns often see an exodus of folks every year. People of all ages are often hungry for experiences that can seem impossible to find in well-known, even well-loved, places. The place where everyone knows their names, and their parents' names for that matter, can lose its luster from time to time.

Some people strike out to make a new way for themselves. Surprisingly— or maybe not surprisingly at all—at some point or another, most hearts find their way back home. Whether it's during a visit to rekindle long- neglected connections or that ache of something missing that makes it apparent, the truth of home always asserts itself. You can leave home, but home will never leave you.

This seems to be especially true of Sault Sainte Marie. It exerts a unique pull over its wandering citizens, beckoning them to come back, no matter how long they've been away. Sault Sainte Marie has often called citizens roaming far and wide to return to build up the economic foundation of our historical community. Recently, this has manifested itself in former citizens returning to the Sault to purchase and revitalize the Sault Sainte Marie Country Club, open a thriving health food store, open an investment-strategy consulting firm, open a microbrewery and winery, and achieve many other successful business ventures. And of course, this pull surely propelled Mike to use his talent for writing to enrich and uplift the citizens of Sault Sainte Marie through his support of the Soo Theatre Project.

The arts are a vital part of all communities, and the Soo Theatre is a celebration of the vibrant community of artists here in Sault Sainte Marie. The Soo Theatre Project has brought opportunities for education, entertainment, and real joy to our community members of all ages while preserving a treasured historical site. Its continued efforts to restore the beautiful Soo Theatre for year-round use will ensure that these opportunities can be enjoyed throughout every season in our northern town, adding to the quality of our community and culture in immeasurable ways. This has been an enormous undertaking, contributed to substantially by dozens of our citizens who, together, are meeting a real need in our community.

The richness of community comes from all people who love it—from those that live within our city limits or across the country. Sault Sainte Marie is continuously shaped both by the people who gather here and make this place their home and by those individuals who invest their energies in their hometown community from a distance.

These investments and the culture it shapes will certainly mold the community as it progresses further through the coming years and will also support the wide variety of resources put into place to support stable and steady growth. These resources, including Lake Superior State University, the city's industrial incubator buildings and air industrial park, the international atmosphere, our health and wellness infrastructure, and many other assets, are sustained through this sense of community and reinvestment.

Indeed, the cultivation of community character and reinvestment will provide vital support to the continued and noble work of stitching together our warm and vibrant community. From this work, it can be assured that future generations will love our home as much as we do.

Anthony G. Bosbous,
Mayor of the City of Sault Sainte Marie, Michigan

Statement

All proceeds from the sale of my book, *The Sounds and Smells of My Childhood—Part II*, will once again be donated to the Soo Theatre Project Inc., a 501(c)(3) nonprofit corporation organized to bring the cultural arts to the people of the Sault Sainte Marie community.

Introduction

"Come Home, Mike McCarthy, to Me"—I'm Still a Son of the Sault

Let me tell you a secret: the garden of Eden still exists; it hasn't vanished. Drive up I-75 going north, as if you're driving to Canada, then turn right at the International Bridge Plaza, and drive over the hill. There you will find it: Sault Sainte Marie.

Have you ever thought about how many different countries and how many different cultures refer to their native land as a woman? For example, look at Mother Russia or Lady England. Ireland itself has made reference several times of calling Ireland by a woman's name and even as an "old woman." My Dark Rosaleen and Cathleen Ni Houlihan are other names as well. Here in the Unites States, our flag is called old glory; our Statue of Liberty is called Lady Liberty. In our hometown of the Sault, French explorers named our river after our Blessed Mother hence the St. Mary's River and our own Sault Sainte Marie.

In my lifetime, I have come full circle in my love of the Soo. Growing up in the East End of town, I so loved it. I really knew this place, and it seemed in every house in my neighborhood, I knew someone. I was educated here and started my career here. I was very passionate about my work to help people. Recruiting and developing new jobs so people could live here fit me right to the core of who I was. But I also felt its meanness, its hardness, and its raunchy politics. But age and maturity settled in with all my career moves. And with it, so too did the value of what I learned and experienced in my hometown. It helped me succeed in cities like Dayton, Columbus, and Denver. Slowly, I began my own change, and my deep regard for the love and kindness of the people of the Soo started to have its impact. I finally grew up. To me, Sault

Sainte Marie became a beautiful, proud, lovely old woman. Sure, wasn't it the home of my grandmothers, my mother, Verna Lawrence, Sr. Mary Quinn, and my lovely aunt Doine? These were women who mattered to me and whom I deeply respected and loved. Do you know what I mean when I call the Sault a beautiful, proud, lovely old woman? Come to the Soo, and see it for yourself. Stand by our beautiful St. Mary's River, which runs from our rapids—so very clear and free. You will feel it, find it, and see it firsthand. Life is more than a song. We have our northern winds that keep our breeze fresh, pure, and clean. Sure, we love to tell our stories, and everyone has one. We know our past has been lost, but we look forward to our future. It's not only the resilience of the people that I admire—I so enjoy—that here, we have a humor that's not found everywhere. At least not in my travels, and I have traveled plenty. At times, it's cold, and yes, the winters can be long, but if it's warmth you want, friendship here matters, civic pride and involvement are easy and free, and the community is open, not closed. That's important for a young family; I know that personally. If one who wishes to move here wants that kind of society, it's here, it's here. Here we have hope. These traits, to me, all represent a beautiful, proud, lovely old woman who is happy in her own skin and loves this place.

> My mother once told me that when I was born,
> The day I first saw the light.
> I looked down our street of my very first morn,
> And gave a great howl of delight.
>
> Now most newborn babies appear in a huff,
> And start with a horrible squall,
> But I knew I was born in Sault Ste Marie,
> And that's why I smiled at them all.
>
> In tones that are tender and tones that are rough,
> Come whispering over the sea.
> Come back Mike McCarthy to Sault Ste. Marie,
> Come home Mike McCarthy to me.
>
> *(Percy French, a song of Irish emigration)*

I went back home and had a very successful book signing at the Soo Theatre. Their leadership is truly committed. Their mission is to see the theater take its rightful place once again as the centerpiece of cultural entertainment for the Soo and region. Being with them, I found it easy to be committed, and I stand with them, committed today. When I returned back to my home in Colorado, I began in earnest to research and write ideas and thoughts to pull together part 2 of *The Sounds and Smells of My Childhood*. Since the publication of my first memoir, friends and family have asked me to continue writing. I have always viewed myself as a storyteller. Raised by an Irish father, who raised me in the oral tradition, my mother—God love her—always seemed to communicate with me through poetry, even as a young boy. They must have known or seen something—a little different with their second son. I never saw myself as a writer as my sister Mary did. But I must say how much I enjoyed writing down those wonderful memories. It is as my dad said: "All of the stories are from people we knew and deeply loved, and by telling their stories, we keep them alive and feel them near us." It has been so personally pleasing and rewarding how my book has moved so many readers to fondly remember periods of their youth. Those times have not been discarded as they may have thought, and smiles reemerge when they think back to those times once again.

So I wanted part 2 to be a continuation of growing up in the Soo during the 1950s. Sault Sainte Marie was thriving then; it was exciting—the people, resilient but loving—and very patriotic. It was the ideal place to grow up. The theme of my new book, part 2, will still be based on David Mallett's poem/song, "I Knew This Place," which gave all the original stories life and meaning and humor. My wish is, his poem/ song will do it again.

Additionally, I have asked my two sisters, Mary and Kathleen, and my two dear boyhood friends who grew up as well in the East End, Peter Campbell and Paul Byron, to write a chapter each themselves. We chose these chapters together to give a different point of view to the reader of the same period so they will be writing of their youth, and I appreciate their effort in doing so. Both sisters are excellent writers. In fact, Mary is a successful author and writer, while Kathleen is a successful copywriter and editor at Michigan State University. I am also looking forward to their special collaboration story written about our Grandmother Trempe, a loving, passionate small woman who greatly impacted both my sisters' lives. Gramma had an impact on all the McCarthys, and I hope you will enjoy reading my sisters' chapter. Pete and Paul are two of the best story-tellers I have ever heard, and I'm sure everyone will enjoy their chapters as well.

So once again, and just one more time, I would ask the reader, take this nostalgic journey with me and try to recall once more those sounds and smells of your childhood during the 1950s while I remember mine.

I Knew This Place

I knew this place, I knew it well,
Every sound and every smell,
And every time I walked I fell
For the first two years or so.

There across the grassy yard,
I a young boy runnin' hard.
Brown and bruised and battle
Scarred and lost in sweet illusion.

From my window I can see
The fingers of an ancient tree.
Reaching out it calls to me
To climb its surly branches.

But all my climbing days are gone
And these tired legs I'm standin' on
Would scarcely dare to leave the spot upon
Which they are standin'.

And I remember every word
From every voice I ever heard,
Every frog and every bird,
Yes, this is where it starts.

A brother's laugh, the sighing wind,
This is where my life begins.
This is where I learned to use my
Hands and hear my heart.

This house is old, it carries on
Like lyrics to an old time song,
Always changed but never gone,
This house can stand the seasons.

Our lives pass on from door to door,
Dust upon the wooden floor,
Feather rain and thunder roar,
We need not know the reason.

And all these thoughts come back to
Me like ships across a friendly sea,
Like breezes blowing endlessly,
Like rivers running deep.

The day is done.
The lights are low,
The wheels of life are turning slow
And as these visions turn and go,
I lay me down to sleep.

(David Mallett, "I Knew This Place")

The Sounds of My Childhood

Our St. Mary's River connects two of our Great Lakes together, Lake Superior and Lake Huron. You may recall from my first book, *The Sounds and Smells of My Childhood*, we were a city built on the banks of the magnificent and beautiful St. Mary's River. Sault Canada was our northern neighbor, while we in Sault Michigan were bordered on its southern shore. The city's name was derived from the French term for the nearby rapids, which was called Les Saults de Sainte Marie. Sainte Marie (Saint Mary) was the name of the river, and saults referred to the rapids. In the early 1910s, the population of Sault Ontario was once smaller than ours here in Michigan, but it began to soar in the 1940s, and today, its regional population is close to eighty thousand, while the Soo Michigan regional population is about fifteen thousand.

As the St. Mary's River was ours, it was a part of each of us. We all felt a special bond with Lake Superior and Lake Huron. Many towns around the lakes were either involved with mining or engaged in processing or shipping. Tourism was another significant industry because of the lakes' rugged shorelines and beauty. We who lived on the river or near it or had a residence along their lakeshores knew the difference between "the lakers," and "the salties." Both were freighters, but ours were the large cargo vessels versus the smaller oceangoing ships from foreign ports.

But Lake Superior had a special reputation. It could be your worst nightmare if you were out on it during a storm, or it could be such a pleasant experience. The locals loved the roar of the whitecaps, and you could see them all the way from Brimley Bay, right through to Whitefish Point, and right across the northern shore of the Upper Peninsula. We used to drive to Lake Superior quite often to visit the pines for a Sunday picnic. We all knew Lake Superior was something very special. Our parents told us a bunch of things about the lake, like its original Ojibwa name, Gitche Gumee. It was the largest freshwater lake in the world, and all the Great Lakes could fit into it. The lake was that big. But the size of it always caught my imagination; it was over 350 miles long and 1,300 feet deep. Those statistics were pretty big, I thought.

It was enormously huge. Its northern shore was in Ontario while it was bordered to the south and west by Wisconsin, Minnesota, and our own Upper Peninsula of Michigan.

But Lake Superior was special in other ways too, especially for my family. Lake Superior was a place, it was said by sailors, "where myths were made." Its storms and waves were famous. Our local sailors and people who lived along its shore spoke about them often.

We went there in all kinds of weather. The weather on the lake changed very quickly at times. I remember clearly one Sunday afternoon—it was one of those good days—the beach for miles was deserted. The lake was rumbling perhaps in anticipation of rain or perhaps in response to the wind blowing in our first blast of autumn air. The roar of the waves was nearly deafening. It was that loud. But they were clean and pure. They were powerful too and yet peaceful. There are so many emotions that the sound of the lapping waves bring out, but they will, in fact, calm you. A poet once wrote, "The roar of crashing waves against the rocky coast will touch your soul. And the cool early autumn air will refresh you with every deep, restorative breath." He was talking about his state of Maine, but that was the way it was in Lake Superior that special day for our family.

It rumbled like a huge drum. We enjoyed listening to the roar of the whitecap waves, and the whistle of the wind in the pines was going on all around us. Pieces of driftwood would be rolling in onshore from the heavy waves. We had so much fun trying to dodge the huge waves as they rolled up to the sand near our picnic area. You could see dead branches all over the shore. We still wished our parents would buy this location. We all so loved it.

A roar of waves like that brings back fond memories of my childhood. Those moments and the pictures of those days and places along Lake Superior are alive in my memory still. There is just one word to describe them: wow!

> I will arise and go now, and go to Innisfree,
> And a small cabin build there, of clay and wattles made; Nine
> bean-rows will I have there, a hive for the honey-bee, And live
> alone in the bee-loud glade.
>
> I will arise and go now, for always night and day
> I hear lake water lapping with low sounds by the shore; While I
> stand on the roadway, or on the pavements grey,
> I hear it in the deep heart's core.
>
> (W. B. Yeats, "The Lake Isle of Innisfree," *The Collected Poems of W. B. Yeats* [1989])

Those of us who are from here, as well as those of us who have adopted this place, will agree that our hearts belong to this lake. It is the lake of our mothers. There is nothing like the roaring of the lake; it is more than soothing—it is a lullaby. Have you heard it? Have you been there and seen it? Have you smelled the freshness of these waves and the chill of the pine-scented air? These are just some of the sounds and smells of my childhood. Do you remember yours?

First Chapter of the Sounds

1. "Let the Cat Die Down"

We called my fathers' parents Pop and Ma. They were our Irish grandparents. They had a lovely farm in the country we used to visit. Pop and Ma kept the original land that Pop's family had homesteaded. They homesteaded in a place called Tone. Grandpa Hassett named Tone, Michigan. He was Ma's father. He set up the first post office there in 1897 in honor of the Irish patriot Theobold Wolfe Tone, and it remained there until it was relocated to the current post office in Kinross. We fondly called where Pop and Ma lived the Farm. It was located seventeen miles east of the Soo and about four miles outside of the small rural village of Pickford. My father and his sister Doine were raised there and went to public school there. In its time, the farm yielded crops to sustain life and had two barns with plenty of hay that fed its animals. When we were there, they had three cows, a team of workhorses, an older horse that we could ride, and some range-fed chickens. It had lovely rolling hills with a great apple orchard our grandmother planted and nursed, with a total of twenty-two different apple trees. But we also had several huge pine trees. It seemed in our youth, it was like our second home. Our McDonald cousins were always there, and it was such a delight playing there, whether in winter or summer. We were always busy doing something, exploring all 160 acres from post to post, picking wildflowers, catching bumblebees, taking the toboggan down the big hills full of snow, and eating all kinds of apples, but the main event was swinging on Pop's homemade swing.

When Doine and Dad were children, Pop built a swing around a large thick branch hanging from the biggest pine tree on the farm. He took the heavy industrial wire that was used to run his portable mill and moved it to different locations. The heavy wire would be used to haul the mill to locations within the forests they were cutting at that time. Horses were used to do the hauling. In the winter, they used large sleds and logs to move their mill. The wire could hold anything; in other words, it was extremely safe. We as kids used to tire Pop out. We could be pushed and pushed on that swing all day. He was so good, and we loved him so much. He never ever got tired, or so we thought. He would push us right to the point we thought we were going to do a complete loop. We all thought for just a brief second we would crash into another huge pine branch. He would then yell out, "Now hold on, but let the cat die down," which was, at times, a relief. No one wanted to be afraid because he pushed all of us so high. But the swing would come eventually to a halt, and the next in line could take a turn. He had great instincts and loved his grandchildren and showed it always. Pop was a pretty cool guy, we all thought.

"Higher, higher, swing me higher, Dad-o!
I can almost touch those leaves with my big toe . . .
I did it! I touched them! Now we can let the cat die, Dad-o."
My white knuckles held tightly to the rope swing.
He would have never "let the cat die"
That only meant he wouldn't push any longer
And I could fall backward when I got brave enough . . .
Right back into his big strong hugging arms.

(Barbara Attaway, "Let the Cat Die Down")

2. Jets, Bombers, and More Jets

The leadership of Sault Sainte Marie never ever lost faith with our air force base in the 1950s, which changed its name from Kinross Air Base to Kincheloe Air Force Base. It was renamed in 1959 in honor of Capt. Ivan C. Kincheloe, who was an air force test pilot, an ace, and a Korean War veteran who was killed in 1958 in California. The air base was located just sixteen miles south of the Soo. Captain Kincheloe was a national hero who gave his life for our country. The locals in Kinross were a little upset as the base was located within their township. However, in time, things became normal once again. The elected leadership of the Sault did everything they could to tap into the new military leadership of the base, as did our business community through our city chamber of commerce setting up its military affairs committee and its committees to assist base families. It worked too as the Soo was always designated by the Department of Defense as being a very supportive community for our country's military. Good grades and reviews like that, plus great performance, allowed constant military investment for the next twenty years at Kincheloe, and that too impacted the town's economy significantly.

As I mentioned, the greatest part of the name change was a boom for our economy. The base expanded in personnel from just a fighting squadron to a combined B-52 bomber squadron, the KC-135 refuelers, and of course, the F-102 fighter jets. Nearly doubling in military personnel meant a lot to our local leaders as well. Dad was a banker then, and the business community welcomed the base expansion.

It also meant an increase in practice air missions throughout the Sault region. The locals sure had to get used to it. We kids noticed the difference right away. Daily, we would hear the big booms, which meant our jets were breaking the sound barrier. We certainly knew our jets were there. The first time we heard a jet breaking the sound barrier, we kids would jump at the sound; it was a very loud boom. Like anything else though, we all got used to it. The pilots would fly all sorts of patterns and at all heights and distances. We really enjoyed their low flight patterns because they seemed to be right up close and right above us. We could see their every move. As kids, we all thought they flew like our Canadian geese did, all of them, flying in perfect formation. I know that sounds crazy now, but that's what we all thought. But these jets were much faster.

3. Snowmobiles Take Over the Soo

It was in February of every winter. The Soo became much like the stories you would read about our Old West. However, instead of lawlessness and horses, we had snowmobiles everywhere taking over the town in preparation of the I-500 Snowmobile Race. The track was located off

W. Easterday Avenue at the north of the I-75 turnoff, the last exit one would take before moving on to the International Bridge Plaza. The I-500 was very unique at the time, and the promoters of it in the city did it up right. Literally, thousands of guests and tourists would come in to town for the weekend and participate in a five-hundred-mile snowmobile race around a one-mile oval track. There were teams that came from every snowmobile manufacturer in our country and many from Canada. These machines were hot, revved up, loud, and ready to race. It was truly our own version of the popular Indianapolis 500 auto race right here in our beautiful little town.

For sure, we always had plenty of snow. And I would bet half the Soo's population came out to see the race. We went there a few times. Each time we did, we saw how passionate people were who followed this snowmobile circuit. We were the granddaddy of them all, and everyone felt great pride in our town's accomplishment. It was really amazing, and it was great fun with snowmobiles everywhere flashing by you or others just taking a pleasure drive. The sounds, however, were loud, and the engines were roaring, and it seemed they were everywhere. Our town was so colorful, I always thought, with all its various-colored snowmobiles.

Our mother really enjoyed herself during our I-500 weekend. As we grew up as kids, she was always the taxi for us. She would jump at the chance to take us to our friends or drive us to a party or even a movie on her own blue Evinrude snowmobile. She really enjoyed herself and got the biggest kick out of it. It lasted the whole weekend of the race. My father, who enjoyed it himself, used to have a good laugh over her behavior.

Everyone was always having a good time with lots of fun; the whole town itself was in a joyous and playful mood. The town was lit up and really showed itself well—that was, until my father got hooked up with his two Irish buddies, Bill Murphy and Ernie Lee. When the three of them got together, you knew what you were looking at, and it was always trouble. They definitely were characters. It was very fitting to call them the Three Amigos. Yet it was funny in a strange way because the storytelling was always so great. The laughter was all around you, but trouble was coming just the same. You see, the three of them were the real owners of the snow machine. No one could convince my mother of that on this special weekend. That snowmobile was hers.

My mother knew well enough that before the three of them took off, she needed to get them a good dinner. She made sure they had their fill. About eight o'clock in the evening, the three of them—after eating and doing their social visit with the family—decided it was time for a ride. Yes, I said the three of them, which immediately was illegal. Dad said not to worry as they would take the back routes and roads to the American Legion Hall for just one drink and would then come home. He assured our mother that he would avoid any police and not get caught. If they did get caught, they would be ticketed. The roads were mostly clear of all cars. There were just snowmobiles out, so the police vehicles could be spotted quite easily. So he told Mom not to worry.

What we all thought could happen came true later in that evening. As I said earlier, these three great friends together were nothing but trouble. I so much enjoyed their free and crazy spirit, their storytelling, and especially the laughter they brought to the family. So when the word came back that they were in a serious accident and were hit by a car on the snow machine, it didn't surprise any of us. We heard how Ernie was thrown from the sled a great distance into a snowdrift. He was not seriously injured from the impact of the sliding car. Bill had a severely broken leg from the collision as the vehicle hit him almost head-on. My father, who was driving the sled, went to the hospital and was treated for severely bruised ribs. Other than that, everyone was OK, Dad said when he called. My father used to call that an Irishman's story. The snowmobile was totaled. We found out later in the police report that the driver of the car was ticketed for DUI, and Ernie was a witness as he walked up to the accident as if he were a stranger. My father wasn't ticketed as there were just two adult men on the sled, and Ernie was willing to testify to that.

The following morning was hilarious as well as tense. But that seemed to be the path for these three most of the time when they got together. We all enjoyed teasing our father about his evening out on the snowmobile. After getting very angry at Mom and all of us for our lack of loyalty, he softened up a bit. He became pretty embarrassed by it all and made his calls to Ernie and Bill to see how they were doing. They still were buddies.

4. Me and Terry Sawchuk

The Detroit Red Wings was one of the six original NHL franchises. They came to the Soo in 1948. When their ownership was announced, "the Soo would be one of two training sites for the team." They indicated in their announcement that the Pullar had the best ice in the country and that there was no better place to train. This certainly aided our town in taking on the brand name Hockeytown USA for years, and we still maintain that brand to this day. This relationship with the Soo lasted for nearly a decade until Detroit built its own facilities for the team in their home location. The team was a big economic hit in the town, especially at the Antler's Bar, where they all seemed to play, and the Ojibway Hotel, where they all lived. The whole town enjoyed having them; they were friendly and a lot of fun.

All the top Wings were there: Sid Abel, Ted Lindsay, Gordie Howe, Red Kelly, Alex Delvechio, Norm Ullman, Marcel Pronovost, and the greatest goalie ever— Terry Sawchuk. I was a goalie at that time in our neighborhood teams, and my hero was the man himself.

It was 1955 when I met him at their training camp. All the Red Wings players took time to meet with the locals always and chatted with us. We got to know some of them and developed some friendships along the way with the team players. My dad had met Terry Sawchuk at the Antler's Bar one evening and had me shake his hand. Dad wanted me to show him where my tooth was knocked out of my mouth with a hockey puck. It was great, and he was so good. He laughed and pulled out his false teeth and showed me the seven teeth he has had knocked out playing in the net. As I looked at him, I saw a real road map, with deep lines and scars over his entire face. He had a total of four hundred stitches from cuts caused by pucks and sticks he took to his face while being the goalie for the Wings. He asked me if it hurt losing the tooth and how it was for me getting back into the net. I felt so proud telling him, "I never left the net. I just put my tooth in my pocket, just in case the tooth fairy was still around, and kept playing." He picked me up and said, "Good boy, Mike. Here, this is for you." And he gave me a quarter. I think somewhere in my things, I still have that quarter. I still think he was the greatest goalie ever.

5. "Just Call Me Boo"—my Friend Freddy

One of my oldest and closest friends through all my childhood and teenage years—in fact, leading right up through our twenties—was a man I knew as a little boy in first grade. I remember him when he was five. He was constantly smiling and always talking—all the time, always. When we were standing in our grade line waiting for the school bell to ring, he would be talking. The rule was, you had to be silent or you will be punished by the sisters, and these women carried large straps. They scared me, but not Freddy.

I always thought he had a way with the nuns. He came from a large French family. All the nuns and priests—really everyone—seemed to know him. Or probably they knew his mom and dad. We had several French nuns in our school. The origin of the Sault was French and Native American, much like my mother's family. The fact that he was French had my mother like him right away. Mom told me the nuns probably taught his older brothers and sisters, and that made sense to me when I asked my mom about him. I told her with some bitterness, "That mattered with the fine Sisters of Loretto." I didn't really like too many of them. And Freddy was smart enough to get it. He knew how to use it to his advantage. I always thought how smart this little guy was, and I really liked him; he was really funny. I can learn from him, I thought.

He always came to school with a basketball in his hands, always dribbling it while he would be talking with you. This boy loved basketball at a real early age, and in the second grade, he made the B team in our grade school basketball program. I always called him Freddy, but after he made the B team, he changed his name to Boo. It was highly unusual for a second grader to make the team of twelve boys. He simply was that good at a young age. You knew when he was coming because you would hear a ball being dribbled behind or around you.

Boo wanted me to try out for the team and join him on the B team as second graders. I told him I knew what a hockey puck was as I was a goalie in the East End, but I could not even dribble the ball. So Freddy—or Boo, as I now called him—began to teach me how to play basketball on the court in our school gym and on the outside playground. Every day at school, he would teach me something new. He never did stop talking, but he never repeated himself, and as I said, he was always smiling. So he was fun. Of course, I tried to listen to his every word because here was a kid who made the B team when he was in second grade. I thought that was big stuff.

Boo had the most interesting shot, I thought. He would cock the ball back to his side and let it fly, and he would make more shots than he missed. You could understand why he made the team.

By the time I was in fourth grade, I went with Boo and three other boys from our class to try out for our basketball team. Our coach then was a man named Russ Payment. He was a small man but had a good reputation of being a solid basketball player and someone who hated to lose. In other words, he wanted to win. My mother liked the fact he was a Payment as that was her mother's name. Her mother, named Mary, was a cousin of Coach Payment's father, Russ Sr. But cousin or not, he was tough—very tough—and you had to put in your time at practice, or he simply wouldn't play you in a game. We had three boys in our grade make the team, and we played for Coach Payment: Boo, another boy called Jimmy Fuerstnau, and myself. Jimmy too was a great kid, but there were two things I felt though that were funny with Jimmy. Everyone at that young age had a difficult time pronouncing his last name, so like all kids do, we gave him a nickname, and we called him Friz. The second thing was, for an eight-year-old boy, he had the largest hands I ever saw; they were huge, and we all knew he could palm a basketball if he wanted to. I think Boo was happier than me when the coach called my name and Friz's. We all played ball through our twenties together, and I always knew where they were on the floor.

The Miracle of Friendship

There is a miracle called friendship

That dwells within the heart,

And you don't how it happens Or even when it starts.

But the happiness it brings you Always gives a special lift,

And you realize that friendship, Is God's most precious gift.

6. New Fort Brady—MTU Soo Branch

Fort Brady was a frontier fort established in Sault Sainte Marie, Michigan, to guard against British incursions from Canada. The original location of the fort, known as Old Fort Brady, was along the St. Mary's River on Water Street. Fort Brady was located at this site from 1822 until 1893, when it was moved to a new location on higher ground, known as New Fort Brady. The fort was located at the new site from 1893 until its close in 1944. The site of Old Fort Brady was designated a Michigan State Historic Site in 1956 and listed on the National Register of Historic Places in 1971. The primary responsibility of the post at New Fort Brady was to protect the canal. Troops from the fort assisted during civil unrest in 1894, and during the Spanish-American War of 1898, two thousand troops passed through the fort for training.

During World War II, fifteen thousand troops lived at Fort Brady, necessitating various temporary and not-so-temporary constructions of habitations and facilities. The Second Infantry Division conducted cold-weather training at the fort to determine what equipment would be necessary.

However, in 1944, even before the end of World War II, however, the army decided to close the fort as surplus. In 1946, the army gave the fort to the Michigan College of Mining and Technology, now Michigan Technology University, who established the Soo Tech branch campus at the site. After renovation, the fort was sold to Lake Superior State College, now Lake Superior State University. Many of the original buildings have been replaced, but the major buildings of New Fort Brady have been well maintained and form the heart of the campus. These buildings are now row houses, the administration building, Fletcher Center, Brady Hall, South Hall, Brown Hall, East Hall, and the childcare center.

During the 1950s, the Soo Tech branch was a great place to go. It had one of the region's best gymnasiums. Some great college and high school games were played there, and I certainly tried to go to them all. Our two local high schools were the Sault High Blue Devils and the Loretto Angels. They often played there. The Soo had some pretty good teams then and, I thought, some good ballplayers too. They played in two different leagues. I found out from my brother the public school was much bigger than the Catholic school was. They never played against one another. We all used to laugh at the school nicknames as we called them the Angels and the Blue Devils. I had become a total basketball junkie at the time and loved seeing the bigger guys play. The best thing, though, was watching the Harlem Globetrotters and Harlem Stars play when they came to town. They were so funny, and they were great entertainers. They really could play basketball when they absolutely had to. Their biggest stars were Goose Tatum and Marques Haynes. There was a great history to their team. It had a lot to do with just the color of one man's skin. Now keep in mind this was the fifties; they were just black basketball players and were not allowed to play in the original National Basketball League, so they created their own team. They toured the country, and everyone just loved them. I didn't fully understand it, as the Soo had black soldiers at Camp Lucas and black servicemen at Kincheloe AFB, and everyone seemed to get along, and everything was good. Our town was very open to people, I felt, so I always asked my older brother, John, why this was happening. He just said, "Don't worry about it, Mike. Just be who you are." So of course, I had to ask my father, and Dad gave me a bit more of a history lesson. I think I was sorry I even asked the question.

But the one time they were playing, and I remember it as if it just happened yesterday, Goose Tatum was standing right by me on the sideline and right at half-court on the floor. I yelled out to him "Two bits!" as his teammate passed him the ball. He looked at me and smiled and said, "You're going to owe twenty-five cents, little buddy," and he took a hook shot at midcourt and swished it. I didn't have the two bits, so he hoisted me up on his shoulders after asking my dad if he could do it and ran around the gym floor holding me, wanting to sell me for the twenty-five cents to any fan who would give it to him. He eventually brought me back to my seat and to my parents, but it was a fun time I will never forget at the Soo Tech campus. (Lake Superior State University Library)

7. The Frogs of Spring

Every spring of the year, Bill Murphy, our father's great friend, would come over to our house in the early evening and take us kids with our dad out for a ride to listen to the frogs. He introduced us to how he and my father were raised as children. When they were young, our country was divided over religion. Quite often, those of the Protestant faith treated Catholics as second-class citizens. That was the case in our town. One of the ways Catholics fought back was through playing silly little childhood games—namely, in the spring, referring to frogs and their sounds in a religious manner. In other words, we had Catholic frogs, and we had Protestant frogs. The Catholic frogs always sounded the prettiest and the most pleasant and always sounded very happy. The Protestant frogs sounded strong and shrill, always angry, as if they didn't enjoy the springtime at all. So we always asked Bill and Dad very innocently, "Was that a Catholic frog or a Protestant frog that just croaked?" This was a standard question until we as kids thought we understood it.

It was normally early in the spring of every year as I said when the snows had left the fields filing the ponds and meadow streams. Likewise, our swamps would be filling back in while the St. Mary's River fog was stirring along the riverbanks, moving throughout the countryside. We could hear them, plenty of them, croaking, barking, ticking, and tapping. I even thought their sound was like my brother John and I having our burping contests.

It was great fun, and we thought we were actually learning something totally new. We studied the sounds and felt we could pick out the Catholic frogs ourselves after going with them several times. According to Dad and Bill, we were developing the ability to identify different kinds of frogs "by ear."

For most people, the call of frogs signals many things such as the change of season or an incoming rain or the warmth of summer. But for us, it was different. It meant to us that we had to identify who had the better frogs. We were Catholics. So of course, we had the better-sounding frogs. We had several kinds of frogs in the Upper Peninsula and our town of Sault Sainte Marie; they were the bullfrog, green frog, gray frog, the wood frog, the chorus frog, and the pickerel frog. Each of them had their own distinct sound, and in the spring, they were plentiful. The bullfrog had the most deep and lovely sound; it was almost like the call of a bull, while the pickerel frog had the shrillest sound ever, and they were poisonous too. It was very easy for us to choose who was the Catholic frog between those two. Then we had the green frog, which we found a lot around our swamps and our rivers; they sounded simple and sweet and gave out a cackle, while the gray frog sounded shrill, almost like a bird whistling at a very high pitch.

It got real funny when Bill and Dad tried to teach us who were the female frogs and who were the male frogs. But we first had to pass their test on Catholic and Protestant frog differences. As I said, they had a wide range of sounds, particularly in their breeding season, and they exhibited many different kinds of complex behaviors to attract mates, to fend off predators, and to generally survive. And sure, Bill would always end our search in frog biology with a brief verse of "The Orange and the Green," which brought us back once again to Dad's and Bill's childhood.

This lovely story can go on for hours as I'm sure they enjoyed it as much as we thought we were learning something special and new.

But to this day, my sisters and I, who were the recipients of this new intelligence, in the spring of every year, will call each other and tell the story of a recent trip we made down the river or over the pond where we heard those beautiful Catholic frogs calling out.

> And I remember every word
> From every voice I ever heard.
> Every frog and every bird,
> Yes, this is where it starts.

A brother's laugh, a sighing wind,
This is where my life begins.
This is where I learned to use my
Hands and hear my heart.

(David Mallet, "I Knew This Place")

8. "The Loseys Are Coming"

It was in 1953 and I was five years old when I first met my cousins from Milwaukee. The two older ones came to the Soo first—Ronnie and Judy. They were our first cousins on our mother's side of the family with her youngest sister, Aunt Betty. There were four of them living in Milwaukee. The older ones came for the first few summers and lived at our gramma's house upstairs at our home on 810 Cedar. It was pretty cool, I thought; while we four McCarthy kids all lived downstairs with Mom and Dad, the Loseys were upstairs with Gramma and Grampa. It was an extended family for sure. My grandparents, especially our gramma, loved us all, and she was happy as could be. Ronnie and Judy were nearly the same age as my older brother and sister, John and Mary. They all enjoyed playing together and found doing things together even more fun. Cousins have a lot in common, and they are fun to be with. Like our McDonald cousins, we grew close and shared a lot of our summers together.

Then in the summer of 1955, all of them arrived on the Soo Line Railroad passenger train. I remember driving in our old Chevy, picking them up at the train station, and meeting Terry and Richie for the first time. Both were about my age, with Terry being a little older and Richie being a little younger. It was going to be a summer of fun, I thought, and it really was. It was the best summer ever.

We had a lot of kids in the neighborhood back then, and whether it was playing baseball at the carbide field or going to the lime piles to ride our bikes and jump the lime hills or playing in the swamp or even hitching the Soo Line train, there were always lots to do. Just on Cedar Street alone, we had Patty Ferraro; Johnnie Raffeale; Ray Cremins; the Dennis brothers, Pat and Mike; Tim and Danny Kinney; Billy Sweet; the Sally brothers, Tommy and Jimmy; and although they were younger than us, the Paris brothers, Benny, Rocco, and Carmine. Their neighbors were the twins, Bobby and Tommy Bourque. On Sova Street, we had our cousins, Mike and Pat Wieneke and Bertie and Carl McKerchie; and the Cobbs, Jay and Ray. Down Maple Street were Butchie DiPasquale, Billy Celestino, Burt Charles, and Pat McKee. Then on Spruce Street, there was Stevie Papineau, Rickie Reinhart, Tommy Willette, Paul Byron, Also, Pat Sterling, Georgie Mattson. Burt and Henry Shipman were also our playmates, and they lived nearby. There was a real neat guy I liked, and he also was John's age, Bobbie Collia. Bobby lived with his grandmother from Italy down on Portage. The Jaros brothers, Al and Ed, were a bit older than all of us, and they lived at the end of Spruce Street with their mom and dad. They became policemen like their father, Al. They were a great family, and they always watched out for the east-end boys and tried their best to keep us out of trouble. Two guys who were lots of fun were Buddy Blixt and Denny Burgess, and they always showed up when we had a good ball game going. They were east-end boys too and good ballplayers and always were fun to be with.

So we had all this going when the Loseys came to the Soo for their summer holidays. You can see why summers were so much fun. Terry took a little bit more risks than Rich and a little scrappier. But Rich was liked by everyone and had the kindest heart and the warmest smile. They both were a lot of fun, but I always thought Terry was just a little more like me, meaning trouble followed him. Ronnie, being the oldest, gave us ten lectures a day, it seemed, and watched over us constantly. He and my brother John were cut from the same cloth, we would say, as they certainly controlled our behavior or tried to, but they did pretty good keeping us out of trouble. Gramma and my mother would tell the two of them to watch over us, and they sure loved Gramma. I really liked how all the Loseys used to call my mother Aunt Fran.

We jumped on several of the Soo Line trains those three to four summers and rode them a few times into the Algonquin area of town then walked to Sherman Park. We would always jump off as the train used to come to a near stop by the old tannery plant. We were telling the stories that the older men would say about the railroad hobos that rode the rails during the Depression of the 1930s and of the magnificent things we thought we were experiencing. We were just three little boys of nine, ten, and eleven and thought so proudly of what we had done, until Ronnie and John found out. You would think the world was coming to an end. Boy, did they get mad. They didn't hit us, but they sure threatened on telling Gramma and Mom if we didn't straighten up. All the Loseys eventually moved to the Soo years later, but for those special summers, they came for their summer holidays on the train and, later, the Greyhound bus. The times were filled with laughter, and boys were just being boys.

9. "Now Shut Up You Kids, The Honeymooners Is on TV"

Every Friday night, my parents loved watching Jackie Gleason and his TV series The Honeymooners. The TV series took place in Ralph and Alice Kramden's sparsely furnished small two-room apartment somewhere in New York City. They were a working-class family. He was a bus driver, and his wife, Alice, was a part-time secretary. The family earned about sixty-two dollars a week. His best friend was Norton, who worked in the sewer in New York City and earned equal pay to that of Ralph. He lived in a similar apartment that the Kramdens lived in, but he lived above them. They often talked to each other, yelling out their kitchen window.

They belonged to the Raccoon Lodge together. They were always lodge brothers with some secret codes they loved to use. My parents roared at almost every word they said. My brother and sisters and I used to look at one another and wonder what was so funny. After we got the idea of the show itself, we began to see that our father acted a lot like Jackie Gleason's character, Ralph Kramden, and our mother a lot like his wife, Alice. Our neighbors across the street were the Dennis family, and Roy Dennis was our father's dearest friend. Well, Roy reminded us so much of Norton.

Then we really started to laugh. Many episodes began with a camera shot of Alice in the apartment, waiting for Ralph's arrival from work, just like how our mother used to wait and hold our dinner for Dad to come home from the bank. The more we thought of it, the show was like their own biography. Then, we all started to get hooked on it. The funniest thing was how we used to try to convince our parents they acted like their TV characters. They thought we were goofy. What my parents always seemed to enjoy was how Ralph was always the apparent underdog. He and Norton were always trying these get-rich- quick schemes to secure a better life for the two of them and their families. They always failed, and none of which succeeded, but they liked the fact that they never gave up.

It reminded us of the two great schemes our dad and Mr. Dennis tried to develop in a separate room of our basement. The first was, Dad and Roy were going to grow their own quality mushrooms for retail sale. Stores and shops throughout Michigan were their target. They priced these higher-quality mushrooms and read how in Detroit this was being done successfully. These folks were apparently making some great money. Dad and Roy spoke to the proprietors in Detroit, and they were encouraged to serve even as a franchise. Keep in mind, our father was a banker then, and Roy was a very busy carpet layer. Their plan was to develop and grow several mushroom beds that required plenty of straw, lots of fertilized earth, constant watering, and special heat lamps that would yield greater growth than the normal mushroom grown for commercial use. They swore this could create a minimum of $1 million of revenue, which, of course, was a lot of money back then. Everything was getting teed up, and everyone was getting excited, but then what happened to Ralph Kramden and Norton happened to Dad and Mr. Dennis: nothing grew, nothing, other than the smell that grew significantly.

The loud laughter could be heard on both sides of our street, and Mother and Mrs. Dennis were right in the middle of it. We kids laughed and laughed, but we were still hoping that these crazy guys would hit it, just once.

The second entrepreneurial scheme was, Dad and Roy were going to start their own minibrewery. Yes, I said a minibrewery, right in our own basement. I'm sure no one thought of the smells that could come from a brewery even if it's a microbrewery or a mini one as Dad and Roy could envision. They did their homework and, with some outside help, developed what they thought was going to be a great beer. They priced out their cost and shared it. They got the sign off our mother and Mrs. Dennis. Then the supplies of malt and hops arrived soon after malted barley, malt sugar, and various yeasts. The coolant systems arrived, but it wasn't the kind of coolant systems one would have today. Don't forget this was 1956. Then with lots of grain and heating up the kettles with two stoves, the boys were ready to begin. And again, just like before, everyone, in both families, was really excited, and we all waited for the outcome.

The smell of the McCarthy-Dennis brewery in our house became so strong it's a wonder why anyone in our family was sober at all breathing all that malt and barley, hops and yeast every day, every minute. We tasted it in our food; we smelled it in the pores of our skin even after we bathed. Dad and Mr. Dennis's brew was a very strong stout, but it was so strong of a stout that only the two of them could or would even want to drink it. The laughter never stopped on that one. But the two of them never gave up thinking of the next deal.

10. Taking Grandma to a Basketball Game

Taking our Grandma Trempe, my mother's mom, to a basketball game was always fun and sometimes very tense because we never knew what she would do. Both my mother and father played basketball when each of them were in high school and enjoyed playing with us in the backyard. Gramma always went to my mother's games, and Mom always said, "She could be a little unpredictable." One day, playing our basketball games, both my brother John and I, saw our gramma at her best. When John, my brother, was in the eighth grade, I was in the fifth grade at St. Mary's Elementary School. She would watch the big kids ("who knew what they were doing") play last, but the little kids ("who just liked to run around too much"), she enjoyed too. I was part of the little-kids bunch that she enjoyed. She got herself involved in every part of my game as if she were the coach herself. The coach of our team, she said, was her cousin, and she knew his father very well. She had to believe this fact gave her some special gift to speak out like she used to do. And she did speak out and did it often.

But first, you have to see a picture of this very strong little woman. She was small, four feet eleven inches tall, but she was a sharp cookie, my mom would say. And she wasn't afraid to stand up to anyone twice her size.

My mother would do her best to calm her and keep her in the stands. My mother would always be gentle with her and very respectful—not demanding—and ask her, "Please, Mom, you're up and down like a yo-yo. Sit back and let the kids play." She would ask her to stay in her seat. My mother was raised in Canada, and she maintained her civility and respect, and she always showed it with her mother.

But Grandma, who was raised by the Ursuline Sisters from the age of two to be a French lady, had a very competitive spirit, and as my father always said about her, "She was a spitfire."

Her mother died when she was nearly two years old and left her and her brother, Clemente, alone with their father, Felix, whom we all called Grandpa Payment. We knew her mother was a small woman, and her name was Rose. She was born in Canada in the Garden River Reserve. She was an Algonquin woman, and our grandmother was always very proud of that. Grandpa Payment was a carpenter, and his family were boatbuilders. The family had left French Canada in Quebec, or New France as it was called, and homesteaded on Sugar Island, founding the little hamlet of Payment on the island. He struggled to raise his two little kids before he arranged in St. Ignace a home with the Ursuline Sisters for our grandmother. This was very commonplace at that time, and people did that quite often. She received a great education with the sisters. One nun especially, she stayed very close with. Her name was Mother Francis; she raised Grandma from when she was still a baby until she was a fourteen-year-old girl and served as her surrogate mother. Our mother, Frances, was named in that nun's honor, and she kept a very lovely picture of Mother Francis on the top of her dresser.

Knowing all this about Grandma Trempe, no one should have been surprised when my grandma ran out onto the basketball floor at one of my games. The opponent was giving us a good shellacking. She first wanted to speak with the referee. Doing that, she then pointed out to him how poorly he was calling the game. The poor referee blew his whistle when Gramma started into him. He called for an official time- out and walked Grandma back to the stands where my mother was waiting for her. The official kindly said to Mom, as he knew her, "Mrs. McCarthy, please keep your mother off the basketball floor. There is a game being played." My grandmother was not going to let that be the last word and comment. She told the referee to "call the game fair and give those little boys a chance." There might have been one hundred people in the stands. It was a local game, not a tournament. It was all supporters of the kids and families attending the game. People really knew everyone. There were really no strangers.

All was going well, and Mother was keeping Grandma under some control. You could still hear her yelling out, but God bless her, she stayed in her seat. Then it all blew up. It was in the last quarter of the game, and we were getting trounced. I was dribbling the ball up the floor when this huge boy playing center knocked me to the floor. The referee missed the foul call.

My grandmother left her seat. She ran out onto the floor one more time and gave the referee a piece of her mind. She said she was going to report him to the state. She was going to do this, and she was going to do that, but she would make certain he would never referee again. I think the funniest part, though, was watching this little woman, all four feet eleven inches of her, wagging her finger at the referee. He was a nice man and very kind and stood over six feet tall.

So what are you going to do when you're a boy of eight and this happens to you? I was so very proud of my grandmother and my mom too with how she handled herself after Grandma was kicked out of the game. The two officials walked Grandma out of the gymnasium with my mom at her side. My mom came back and yelled out to the referees, "Call this game right." Then she politely sat down until the game was finished. She said nothing to anyone and went out of the gym to get Grandma and brought her mother back in to watch the next game. As I think about it now, I was never really embarrassed, but those two women are the women that made me. How lucky I am to have their spirit.

Grandma

I miss her so much;
I wish she was here,
But even though she's gone,
I still hear her whisper "I love you" in my ear.

11. "You Belong in the Choir, Mr. McCarthy"

When I was a fifth grader, my focus was to really improve my basketball game and become a starter with Boo on our junior varsity team. I made the B team as a fourth grader, and the coach played all the kids. I scored a few points that year, which made me feel great. I spent a full summer practicing as much as I could on our basket my father and brother put up on our old barn. So when I wasn't playing something else with the neighborhood boys and there was plenty to do, I was shooting my one hundred shots a day.

One of my elementary school teachers at St. Mary's that year was a nun I really liked, and I felt she really liked me. She was a nun we called our music teacher, and my mother really liked her as she taught music to my older brother and oldest sister. Her favorite saying was "Pronounce each word with your mouth, lips, teeth, and tongue." She called herself Mother St. Thomas More and was assigned to teach the fifth grade as well. She came from a French family, the Arments, and was later known as Sister Deborah Arment, so of course, my mother liked her right away. She had a very pleasant smile and really liked teaching the boys in the class, or so it seemed. Finally, I thought this could be a good year.

The previous four teachers from first grade through fourth grade were OK, but we simply did not see eye to eye. I was one of those kids that found out the hard way—by going to the principal's office quite a few times—that they were the bosses. So my fifth grade was going to be a good year, I felt, and it was.

Mother St. Thomas More was very demanding of me. But she always smiled and didn't wrinkle her face up with her eyes and mouth like so many of her other sisters and nuns did with me. She would tell us how she grew up with three brothers and lots of male cousins. She was playful but still very demanding. I told her how I wanted to concentrate on making the junior varsity team as a starter, and I didn't want to give too much of my time for any other after-school work or activities. She was establishing a vocal choir to compete with other Catholic schools throughout the Upper Peninsula from the fifth through the eighth grades. She wanted me on it and had already spoken to my mother. She said to me, "You belong in the choir, Mr. McCarthy." It was going to be a large choir comprising kids from all the grades, but she was also setting up two separate boys and girls troupes, as she called them, for individual competition. We had several boys my age that had that high-pitch soprano voice that boys have at the ages of eight to twelve. I was one of those boys, and I did enjoy singing. She wanted a group of seven of us to sing "Ave Maria." There were four from our grade and three from the sixth grade that were selected for the group. I couldn't tell her no as my mother had already started her campaign at home and lined up my father to speak with me as well. And that song had some special significance for my mother and grandmother.

We had to travel to Escanaba, which was in the middle of the Upper Peninsula. This is where the competition was held. It was held in the month of May as a celebration to the Blessed Mother. We were the fourth of twelve teams to sing, and each group sang two songs. Each group had to sing at least one song in Latin. Mother St. Thomas More was just beaming from the time we arrived to the time we seven boys hit that stage. We all were very sure she was ready and not frightened a bit. It was her job to lead us as our choral director. We knew one of the songs was "Ave Maria," and we all thought we did that song very well. But we didn't know the other song she was going to select for us to sing. It was causing our team to be a little nervous. She took us aside and told us forty-five minutes before we were going onstage. Our first song would be "Queen of the May." It was a song we practiced every day, and she wanted us to start with it to get us going. We liked the song, and we all felt good about it.

She led us out onto the stage, and her eyes were surely smiling, and she was glowing. God love her. She introduced the team and told the judges our two selections would be "Queen of the May" and "Ave Maria."

She turned and looked at us all from her director's stand, picked up her music stick, and whispered to each of us, "Don't worry about the judges. Sing to the audience." Then she tapped her stick three times on the music stand, and we began to sing. I wish I could remember singing that day because I don't; I just remember the standing ovation of the audience and Mother St. Thomas More still beaming and telling us to take a bow. When all the teams were finished, St. Mary's Elementary School Boys Choir came in second.

So there I was, as a nine-year-old learning how to keep my family and my teacher happy "using God's gift," as my mother would say, while I just wanted to play basketball. But I did make the starting team, and Mother St. Thomas More used to come to all our home games. She was really someone special and worth remembering.

Queen of the May

(A traditional Catholic Marian hymn)

Bring flowers of the fairest, bring flowers of the rarest, From
garden and wood-land, and hillside and dale;
Our full hearts are swelling, our Glad voices telling,
The praise of the loveliest, flower of the vale.

O Mary, we crown thee with blossoms today,
Queen of the Angels and Queen of the May,
O Mary, we crown thee with blossoms today,
Queen of the Angels and Queen of the May.

12. First-Grade Fears

I started out going to a public school for kindergarten at Jefferson School, and it was great. It was just two blocks from our house, just across the railroad tracks. We very seldom had to worry about getting home as we were so close. The only times it created a problem was the trains coming through to the carbide plant. My older brother went there through second grade, but he now was going to a Catholic school run by the nuns. My sister Mary went to Jefferson School also but started in first grade at the same school John was going to. I liked Jefferson School, as all the kids were from the East End, and we played with lots of them. The teachers there were really friendly, and the first-grade teacher, Mrs. Osborne, was really neat, I thought. Mrs. Anderson, our kindergarten teacher, taught my brother and my sister, so by the time I came around, she acted as if she already knew me. I just liked going to Jefferson School. It was our neighborhood school. After finishing kindergarten, my world changed, and it was never going to be the same.

I was heading to a school where my older brother was going and my older sister as well. They were enjoying it and liking it. I privately felt they enjoyed it so much because John was designated at home to be a priest, and my sister Mary was designated by my mother and grandmother to be a nun, one of the sisters. So this school was perfect for them. It was called St. Mary's Elementary School. It was a nice-looking building of brick. It had a nice playground and a gym they called Baraga Auditorium. But they had something else—the nuns, or the Sisters of Loretto as they were called.

These sisters educated our mother when she came from Canada. When her family came to our side of the river, Grandma enrolled her daughters at Loretto. It was an all-girls high school called the Loretto Academy for Young Women.

Some of these girls went on to further their education and went to the convent to become sisters themselves, choosing a religious life and a teaching career. My mother knew many of those girls who became nuns. So this is how her children ended up at a Catholic elementary school. Getting a Catholic education was very important to my parents. If it were my choice, I would have stayed at Jefferson School. So this is the background of my first day in first grade with the nuns.

Everything had rules, and my brother and sister tried to explain how things worked. It was much different from public school, they would say. To both of them, going to St. Mary's school was fun, and they both enjoyed their teachers.

It just wasn't how the teachers looked, as their dress and the habits they wore on their heads would scare any kid, but I thought most of them were just plain mean. But we had to be respectful or we would hear from our mother for a long, long time.

They were supposed to be great educators, and they had a long history of teaching kids in our community. So I went off for my first day of school with all this information. The first thing you needed to do when the school bell rang was to stand in a single line for your grade to be called by the principal, who had a large black belt tied to her side. I knew just one of the boys, Pat Wieneke, my cousin. He too had an older brother and sister that told him what to do and was frightened as much as I was. He too wanted to stay at Jefferson. Once the principal called out "First grade" into the school, you would march to your classroom, and you better be quiet or off you went to the principal's office. The teacher, a nun, was called Mother St. somebody as they all took the name of a saint when they took their final vows. That is how we were supposed to address all of them. She had you assigned to a seat even if you didn't want to sit there. And that's how the morning began. She was polite and told us her rules and what she wanted to achieve and what she expected from us. She was going to be teaching us in her class for the entire school year. She would address all her students as mister or miss. She was talking and rambling on and answering our questions, and I just didn't like where I was at. I started to get real scared. I ran out of the classroom and ran up and down the hall of the school, calling for my sister Mary, who was in the second grade. Mary had told me that morning where her room was and how close it was to the first-grade class. I found her classroom and ran into it and sat beside her until she and her teacher could calm me down. As they say, this too shall pass. It just never did for me until the fifth grade.

The funniest thing, though, that happened was many years later. I brought my little brother Tim to the same school for his first grade and for his first day of school. He did the very same thing I did years earlier. Not only did Tim run out of the school; he ran all the way home. I was home but going out the door to a college class, and he met me there. He too was just five. Is it something in the bloodline, maybe?

13. The Joy and Excitement of Our Saturday Gathering at the Pullar

By Mary McCarthy

Who didn't love the Pullar? When I was a young girl growing up in the Soo, a high point in my life was ice-skating on Saturdays at the Pullar Stadium. We didn't have many social outlets outside of family and neighbors—no devices to seek out our own entertainment. My favorite haunts were the Carnegie Public Library, the fountain at the Soo Locks Park, and occasional movies at the Soo and Temple Theatres. But the Pullar was, by far, the most exciting place to be.

My friends on the east end of town—Connie Jaros and Roberta DiPasquale—and I would meet up with friends from the other side of town—Barb Hallesy, Doreen Roy, Karen Fabry—and skate together.

I remember the combined smell of wet socks of hockey players, popcorn, and Zamboni exhaust that would hit my nose when we entered the ice rink area. The wet cold of the ice had a certain smell as well. All of us or some of us would hold hands skating shakily in a circle around the rink, trying to stay upright as boys screeched and scraped by us in their hockey skates. We wore figure skates, of course—beautifully white over-the-ankle skates with dangerous tips. These inevitably had to be trimmed for us rooky figure skaters. We could skate in the middle of the rink, only for doing our tricks or figure skating forms such as twizzles and spirals. We also took great delight in playing "crack the whip" and "cross over hands twirl."

My mother signed me up for figure skating lessons with my cousin Judy when I was about seven. We even performed a number with the older girls from the

Hiawatha Skating Club. I remember Bridget Kinney, my figure skating idol, as she glided around the rink doing her lifts and twirls. But it was the music—the organ music—that enthralled me. We only heard organ music at St. Mary's Church, but this was different! It was peppy . . . zippy . . . romantic even. It was the kind of music that carried us on its sound waves around that frozen ice and stayed in our heads long after we left. Intermingled with the organ music was the sound of the wooden gates slamming as kids entered and left the ice when the voice over the loudspeaker announced "Backward skate" or "Couples skate."

We had fun. We had our version of adventure and excitement. That was reflected in a tune the organ music piped out as we glided and slipped across the ice:

> If you go down to the woods today
> You're sure of a big surprise.
> If you go down to the woods today
> You'd better go in disguise!
>
> For every bear that ever there was
> Will gather there for certain,
> Because today's the day
> The Teddy Bears have their picnic.
>
> See them gaily gad about.
> They love to play and shout,
> They never have any care;
> At six o'clock their Mommies and Daddies
> Will take them home to bed,
> Because they're tired little Teddy Bears.
>
> (Jimmy Kennedy, "Teddy Bear's Picnic")

The Pullar, as we locals called it, held us securely in its own energy field—one created by countless skaters and dreamers. The Pullar was our community-gathering place, a safe haven for us kids.

14. Hockey in the East End

by Reverend Peter G. Campbell

How It Started

I grew up in a city that loved hockey. That love of the game was felt very strongly in each of the neighborhoods in our town. It allowed us kids to develop relationships with one another, our neighborhood, and our city, which have lasted a lifetime. The game and the friendships it has spawned provide an emotional thread that ties me to my roots. The depth of that thread has surprised me. It brings up strong memories of friends who have passed on and those whom I am still connected to around the country. It has been a pleasure reminiscing about the place I call home. I am thankful that Mike McCarthy helped awaken my past to how good the sights, sounds, and smells of my youth really were. What a lovely gift this has been.

The Start

My dad, Gordon "Hump" Campbell, was a hockey guy! I have pictures of him as a young man in the 1920s on an outdoor rink. He stayed involved in the game of hockey as a player, coach, and then general manager of the Sault Indians in the late 1950s. He stayed involved as my main fan until he died in 1964. He wanted me to play the game he loved, but he wasn't pushy about it. In fact, he kept me out of organized hockey as long as he could. He believed I would benefit from skating on the neighborhood outdoor rinks than by playing for a team. I disagreed! I badgered him relentlessly for several years until he gave in and let me join my friends on the East End Junior Peewee team when I was ten years old. Of course, he was right. Because I had been learning how to skate, stickhandle, and shoot outdoor for the last five years, I started right out on one of the top lines.

My First "Real" Skates

My first pair of good hockey skates was used almost to the point of extinction. The Planets Skate Company made them. The blades had been sharpened down to about an eighth of an inch, and they had been coated with layers of cracked shellac to keep them from getting wet. They were beautiful! The previous owner was Harry "the Cat" Vincent. Harry worked at the Sault's venerable Pullar Stadium and was well-known for his speed and grace while skating. Most of the ice maintenance in those days was done while wearing skates. They cleaned the ice with wide push shovels while on skates and pushed a heavy barrel on wheels to resurface the ice. He was a sight to see when he monitored public skating sessions too. He had a certain flair that all we kids aspired to as skaters. Harry was a powerfully fast skater. In fact, it was said he beat the great Gordie Howe in a race around the rink during a Detroit Red Wings training camp. I have paid a lot of money for skates over the years, but my best pair was free!

There were a couple of reasons that Harry Vincent's skates had been worn down so low. First, he was on them a lot, and knowing Harry, he would want them sharp. Second, he had access to sharpening right where he worked. The Pullar had a sharpening machine in the north side of the rink in the vicinity of the rear entrance under the stands. It was about the size of a small bedroom closet. I remember Manny Boucher sharpening skates and an older gentleman named Bill Matheson. I can remember him bent over the sharpener, sparks flying and clouds of carbide steel filling his cubicle. It was hard to breathe even standing outside the half door to the room while the blades were whittled down during sharpening.

The Neighborhood Rinks

We had quite a few outdoor rinks in our neighborhood in the 1950s. I lived in the ten hundred block of Maple Street. Right across the street on Maple was the Bowers's rink, which, in the summer, also was a hot spot for horseshoes. This was a mixed rink in that some time was allotted to hockey and some to figure skating. It had lighting for evening skating, which consisted of a couple of light bulbs attached to wood poles. Mr. Bowers made the rink and maintained it. We were expected to do our part and shovel the snow. The Bowers had two boys, Ed and Dave, and two girls, Nancy and Carol. Some sharing of ice time was necessary. Babe Bowers was the referee for ice time and the hostess when it was time to get warm. This was the only rink I remember being able to walk in the house with skates on to warm our feet. She welcomed us in the house, but when it was time for the girls to skate, we were to drop our sticks or get off the ice. When she bellowed at us, we listened. Most of the time, we just crawled over the fence and went to the Tadgersons' rink on Cedar Street.

The Tadgersons' rink was a little more hockey oriented. Mr. Tadgerson built boards on the end behind the goals. The goal nets were made of two-by-four framing and chicken wire. They were very cool when you were used to digging the puck out of a snowbank after each shot. You only had to chase the puck in the snow when it was deflected or if you could hoist it high enough to go over the top. You might wonder why anyone would want to shoot high enough to go over the top of the boards, but it was very important to be able to hit the upper corners of the goal or top shelf, "where Momma keeps the cookies." The Tadgerson boys, Charley and Tom, were a little younger than most of us, but the availability of ice and the endboards were a big draw when looking for a place to play.

One block to the south on Spruce Street was the Mrozeks' rink. Mr. Mrozek would be my first coach when I joined the East End Juniors. Several years later, this was another rink divided by hockey and figure skating. The brothers Butch and Teddy were pushing hockey, while their sister, Glynice, was the figure skater. And once again, the father was the rink maintenance person; and the mother, the disciplinarian. Cleaning the ice first thing on a Saturday morning, I used the broom to write a risqué word on the ice surface. Being a good Catholic schoolboy, I sometimes liked to push my boundaries! Glynice turned me in to Mrs. Mrozek. I was suspended for all on-ice activities for two weeks. Luckily, I had other options. The ten hundred blocks of Maple, Cedar, and Spruce had three rinks almost with snowball-throwing distance. In a few years, there would be rinks on Portage added to the mix. The Welches and the Martins both had rinks as their kids became of age.

The city of Sault Sainte Marie usually made a big rink at Jefferson School and even had one on the southwest corner of Spruce Street and Shunk Road for a while. These were located close to fire hydrants for watering purposes. In the late fifties, the Muessel family transferred to town in the coast guard. Now, they had a big rink! It was across their backyard and into the Abrahamsons' yard. Boards all around and well lit, it was big enough that it was cleared after snowstorms by a coast guard gray-colored tractor. Both the Muessels and the Abrahamsons had boy and girl skaters, and it was a fun place to play.

The Neighborhood Bond, Road Hockey

There were a lot of elementary school–age kids in my immediate neighborhood in the 1950s. Winter was a marvelous time then. Maple and Cedar Streets had little traffic, making them perfect for road hockey. They had enough streetlights for nighttime games too. Big snowbanks and hard-packed, slicked roads were the norm. These were great conditions for road hockey and hooking cars. The activities often intermingled. In those days, cars had bumpers you could actually grab and "hook" a ride on until you fell off or an adult yelled at you to let go. Adults didn't seem to see the adventure in this that we did. There was never any problem getting a road hockey game going. All it took were two kids shooting a puck back and forth, and then, like magic, others would show up. In those days, we seldom used the phone to find out what our friends were doing; we just looked out the window. Our parents highly encouraged outdoor activity. Before you know it, there would be ten or twelve little Gordie Howes stickhandling and shooting, developing the skills that would come in handy later on. Of course, there were often the little Ted Lindsays too, getting good at smashing people with sticks and elbows to slow them down. They helped the more skilled players learn how to eat snow in the snowbank when they were getting too fancy for our tastes. Squabbles developed on a regular basis, but they usually worked out fairly quickly. If they didn't, the combatants went home until the next day, and they would try again—the East End form of détente!

If we were using pucks, no one volunteered to be the goaltender. There were two reasons. Pucks are made of hard rubber, and they hurt! And if the shooter missed the goal (which was usually two lumps of snow), the goaltender had to chase the puck. How far he traveled depended on the strength and prowess of the shooter. In the beginning, there was more stickhandling and passing involved in scoring goals. When slap shots came into fashion, pucks started flying all over, and the goaltender had to go much farther to retrieve it. If he was unlucky enough to stop the puck, well, that didn't work out well either. Snow pants, or jeans on warm days, were not the best protective equipment.

If a rubber ball or tennis ball was used in place of a puck, we were fighting to play goaltender. Chopper on the stickhandle and tight leather glove jammed in a baseball mitt, we would be doing splits and kicking out shots left and right. Missing meant chasing the ball a long way because balls seemed to bring out more hard slap shots. We imagined we were the NHL's Terry Sawchuk or Jacques Plante or maybe even Terry Hoath or Jimmy Couvier—noted East End goaltenders at the time. Today, there is talk about an oversize goalie hurting the number of goals scored in a game. Back then, we worked the equipment angle too. If your rubber galoshes were five-buckle arctics or zip-up boots, you left them unbuckled or unzipped. You left your bulky wool coat on no matter the temperature. We looked for any advantage to thwart our adversaries, much like how the goaltenders of today try to give themselves an edge. Road hockey brought our little part of the East End together in the winter. Most of the children there went to Jefferson Elementary School, but some of them ended up going to St. Mary's Parochial School. But after school, there was the clack, clack of puck on stick and young voices raised in excited fun. The scene of the game acted as a magnet extending to the neighborhood as we came together. My little pod on Maple—from Elm up to Jo and the Gadys and Cannelos' store in midblock, including the Monroes, Bowers, the Killiips next door, Bobby Bugno, and the Gadys across the street—grew in size. Cedar, Spruce, and Portage Streets joined us: the Perthes boys, the Kelleys, Benoits, and Mrozeks, to name a few. Some of us were closer than others, but we did have a bond of our history together.

The Road Trips

I had two memorable road trips in my youth, which were apart from playing in the Sault Amateur Hockey Association. Both involved growing through embracing pain while having great fun! I don't know who got us to walk all the way from the East End to play a street hockey game in the west end of town. But I would assume it was Charlie Perthes, who seemed to know everyone in town. Charlie was very outgoing, not very tall and had thick glasses. He was a good hockey player, better on his feet than skates. And he was fearless. So it makes sense that he would be the one to get us to play the likes of Big Kenny Lewis and his brother Chester, the McKerchies, Jimmy Sears, and the like. Even though we had added to our lineup this time by adding Albert and Wayne Goetz from farther down Spruce Street, we started off at a huge disadvantage. It was a long trek to the opposite end of town. Luckily, Charlie didn't know anyone in the Algonquin area, which was farther yet. We arrived in much the same condition as Alexander's troops after crossing the Alps. We were whipped before we got there. We were thrashed completely. They were big and strong and played what could be called a very physical game. We enjoyed that type of game also, but they took it to another level. I use the hyperbole of being tired from our long journey to get there as an excuse only. There has to be a reason for the hit our East End pride took that day. We sneaked home to lick our wounds. I believe we laid the whole blame for the fiasco on poor Charlie.

We waited a few years for our next road trip. And this time, we smartened up enough to get a ride from some of our parents. It's a good thing too because it was about ten to fifteen below zero! This time, we traveled to the South Side to play on a splendid rink Bob Quinn made on the end of Young Street by Marquette Avenue. The rink was a big one, much like the Muessel rink in our end of town, and stretched over several lots. It had boards all around and was well lit for our nighttime game. Mr. Quinn was a carpenter, and everything was top-notch.

Some of the parents were fearful of frostbite because of the cold and windchill factor caused by skating. Mr. Quinn made sure they felt at ease by showing off the warming area and supplying materials to ward off the windchill. Old newspapers were stuck underneath our coats to cover our chest, and magazines protected our shins from pucks and cold both. The game was on! I don't remember the score. All I remember is that it was very fast and that it was very rough to play. The South Siders had some good players. Patty Russo, Paul Allen, Dave Marble, Steve Werve, and the Poliski brothers all provided a mixture of skill and toughness. I think their secret weapon, though, was little Robbie Quinn. A little guy like that wasn't supposed to be that good. I can see why his dad built him a rink!

We played under the stars with the wind whistling by our toque-covered heads. We played with abandon, retreating often to the heated porch to get warm. After, we stayed for Mrs. Quinn's hot chocolate and regaled one another with braggadocio of our both real and imagined skills. We did all this, then we silently nursed our bruises. As I said, they had both skill and toughness. What a glorious night!

What a Gift!

I've always loved hockey. I still love hockey. I enjoy the speed, skill, and beauty of the game. I still love to play the game of hockey. Speed is no longer much of a factor in the game I play. But I can still pass the puck, shoot the puck, and know how to anticipate other players' moves. It is a great form of exercise. As strange as it sounds, skating is easy on my body. It has a rhythm and smoothness that lets me move enough to keep in a semblance of good shape. Getting up after falling takes longer than it used to, and it can be rather jarring. I try not to do that too often. I will play until I can't. When that happens, I will turn to my other favorite sports activity. I will be a full-time armchair hockey coach. I will be able to do that right from my recliner in my living room. I practice the position part-time now with my friends Charlie Perthes and Ron Barkley. Maybe, when I take it on all the time, the Red Wings coaching staff will begin to listen to our complaints.

A couple of years ago, I played in an over-sixty tournament in Ellenton, Florida, which is close to Tampa. I played with a team from Minnesota, where I now live. We made it to the championship of our division and came in second. But the highlight of the tournament for me was playing against the Hembroff brothers,

Doug and Ron, who played on a Detroit team. The Hembroffs grew up in Dafter, just outside the Soo. It would be close enough to be called a suburb, if the Soo was big enough to have a suburb.

Not too often do you see hockey players hugging one another before a game. Jeez, I was happy to see them!

15. A Crazy Bunch

by Donald Paul Byron

When the phone rang, I was up to my elbows in soapy water doing dishes. I was surprised to hear Mike's voice when I answered as he was in the Soo just a couple of weeks before and we were able to talk then. Because Christmas was right around the corner, I thought he was just calling with season's greetings. Boy, was I wrong! Dropping a bombshell on me, he asked me to "guest author" a chapter for this book. I couldn't help but wonder if he'd lost his mind. Didn't he remember what kind of a student I was? Those poor nuns that taught us had to turn to coercion in order to get me to turn in a simple essay most of the time. I almost said no to Mike's request but didn't. So now I'm wondering if I haven't lost my mind as I head into unchartered waters, praying I can stay off the rocks.

Wondering what I could write about, I decided to go with a few events and situations I experienced, along with the friends that I made over the years. Matching individual names to some of the things would be darn near impossible as they were done repeatedly and the "cast of characters" wasn't always the same.

When I was attending school, the Soo had two Catholic elementary schools: St. Mary's and St. Joseph's, more commonly called St. Joe's, plus a Catholic high school, Loretto, in addition to the public school system. A student wasn't required to be a Catholic to attend one of the Catholic schools, nor was it required you attend one if you were Catholic. It was the parents' choice.

St. Mary's took in the students who lived north of Easterday Avenue, while St. Joe's served those who lived south of Easterday, which roughly divided the town in half. With that, their students were in a unique situation: instead of meeting and making friends from the smaller area a public school served, the students at St. Mary's and St. Joe's were able to get to know others from literally half the town.

When it came time for me to start elementary school, my parents made the decision to enroll me in St. Mary's. And it is a decision that I have to thank my parents for making. It was one that led to friendships that began while attending St. Mary's and I have been blessed with having to this day.

There isn't a lot to say about my early years at St. Mary's. I don't remember any earthshaking things that happened. Things were done at home in about the same fashion as my friends, and other than the obvious religious aspect and having nuns for teachers, I don't think school life differed much from the public schools. So I guess I led a normal schoolkid's life. But then between sixth and seventh grades, unknown to my younger sister Karen or myself, our parents began looking for a larger house as our family was going to be graced with a new member, our youngest sister, Lori.

I can't remember how or when I found out they were looking for a new house, but when I did, I don't think the idea of moving thrilled me that much. They hadn't made their minds up yet and still were looking, so I was a little concerned they might buy a house in an area where I'd have to transfer to St. Joe's. If they did, I'd be leaving my friends at St. Mary's, along with ones I had in my neighborhood.

Fortunately, the house they ended up buying was in the East End. That ended my concern of transferring as I'd be staying at St. Mary's, and there was a bonus in it for me too: the guys I spent so much time with at St. Mary's such as Pete Campbell, Tim Kinney, Dave Monroe, and Mike lived in the East End. In addition to these guys, there was Charlie Perthes, whom I met through Pete, along with another friend, Rick Reinhart. Simply put, it would be a new neighborhood to me, but I wouldn't have to find new friends in it; my friends were already there.

By then, our boundaries had expanded, and the time to be in at night was later. With the extra time on our hand after supper, we had to find something to do outside, even in the winter. After all, who wanted to be cooped up inside all night?

Playing Road Hockey, Hooking Cars

A good deal of that time in the winter was taken up by playing road hockey. Nearly all winter, the conditions were great for it; the streets stayed covered with a very slippery layer of packed and highly polished snow. It was unusual to see any pavement showing because the only places they used to salt back then was at the intersections of the main streets. We normally played at the intersection of the side streets of our neighborhood. The reason we played at the intersection was they had the best illumination for playing at night.

The equipment needed to play was minimal; it consisted of a hockey puck, and each player needed a hockey stick, and the goals were simply made of mounds of snow. Because of this, it was a great game for the basketball players among us too as they didn't have to know how to skate even. Being competitive in nature, they would be there hooting, hollering, and hacking away with as much gusto as anyone. If I had a dollar for every hour we were out there on those winter nights, I'd be sitting on Easy Street. Those side-street intersections where we played road hockey at night put us in the perfect position to engage in another "winter sport" known as hooking. Unless you're around my age, it's highly possible that you've never heard of it before or ever seen it done, so I'll try to describe how it was done. When a car came to the intersection you were playing road hockey at, it usually would come to a stop or slow down to make a turn on the slick street. When they did that, it allowed you to run up to the rear of the car where you would hook (grab) the bumper while you settled into a squatting position; if your timing was right, this would happen just as the car was pulling away from the intersection. Then you'd go sliding along on your feet for a ride of a block or so, and then you would let go of the bumper so you didn't have too long of a walk back to your corner. That slick covering on the street would allow you to go quite a distance if you wanted. You could tell if someone was a beginner; they wouldn't pay attention to how far they had gone and would hang on too long.

Was it dangerous? Not really. You must remember this was at a time when nearly all the businesses in town closed between five and six o'clock for the day. And most people went home after work, and that was where they stayed until the next morning, so there wasn't a lot of traffic. As matter of fact, at times, there might have been only four or five cars going through the intersection in the course of the evening. Probably the biggest concern was over having a wet chopper stick to one of those big chrome bumpers those old cars had. For those that don't know what a "chopper" is, it was a fairly thick but supple leather mitten under which a heavy woolen mitten was worn. They came in pairs, and the leather mitten was formed to fit the right or left hand. Anyhow, having one stick to a bumper wasn't a big problem in itself. If it did happen, you would just slip your hand out of it and watch it wave goodbye as it sped away with the car. Where the real danger came in was when you got home and had to come up with some kind of excuse to explain why you now had only one chopper.

Every so often, after we'd hooked a few cars, a patrol car with one of the older cops in it would pull up where we were playing road hockey. Motioning us over to the car, he'd ask us if we were hooking cars or if we knew who was doing it. Of course, we'd lie through our teeth, denying any knowledge of it. You could tell those old guys knew what the answer would be before they even asked because with a knowing smile, they'd just nod when we answered, then they'd give us a little warning and explain they were there because some motorist called the station. Then they'd leave. Truthfully, I don't think they were all that concerned about it; I wouldn't doubt that they had done it themselves when they were our age.

One night, though, we got a little surprise. On this particular night, a patrol car pulled up, but instead of one cop in it as usual, there were two. There was a young one, probably a rookie, who was driving and one of those older guys in the passenger seat. We knew the drill, so we gathered around the passenger side of the car. The older cop went through the obligatory questions and warnings. When he finished, we thought they'd leave. The younger one just sat there, not saying a word the whole time, so I thought he was just observing how the older guy did things. But no, it didn't work that way. When the old guy finished, this young one finally spoke up, almost going ballistic, saying he didn't believe us, calling us a bunch of hoodlums, and he was going to keep an eye on us, but the best one was his parting shot when he said we had better watch our step and if we didn't, he'd have our ass. It seemed like the more he talked, the more excited he got. In a way, it was hilarious; it still reminds me of the television character

Barney Fife when he was trying to show his importance and authority. After he finished his little tirade, they finally left. Did it stop us from hooking cars? Sure did for a night or two!

Throwing Snowballs at Cars

Snowballing cars was another big winter activity, and we had a perfect spot for it. About a block east of my house on Spruce Street was a pretty long piece of vacant land that went from Spruce to Carrie Street in depth. It was heavily wooded and had three trails going between Carrie and Spruce Streets. The trails were used as shortcuts year-round, which left the snow packed down in the harshest winters even. Spruce Street, being a main thoroughfare, provided us with ample amount of targets to test our throwing skills.

Because the woods grew right out to the sidewalk, you were able to stand back on the trail just a few feet and have a good view of the street in both directions but still be concealed by the trees. Most of the time, when your snowball hit a car, the driver wouldn't know where the snowball came from because they were focused on the street ahead of them. Every so often, a driver would stop and run into the woods a little way on the trail, but by the time they got stopped on the slippery street, we'd have a head start on them and be long gone.

I think more drivers called the police about this in comparison to hooking cars as it seemed like they showed up a bit more. But when they did, the woods and trails became our allies again. With the big old "bubblegum machines" on the cop cars' roofs and the view we had of the street, you could spot a cop car coming a half block away. When that happened, we'd just go back to the middle of the woods or to the edge on the Cedar Street side. Then we'd quietly wait to see what they were going to do, which was fairly predictable. Sometimes, they'd just circle the block once or twice; other times, they would try scanning the edge of the woods and trails with their car's spotlight, trying to get a glimpse of anyone. It never worked though; we were back in the woods too far for that to be effective. But strange as it may seem, they never came into the woods to look for us, although I can't say I blame them either. Who in their right mind would want to get out of a warm car on a winter night then go traipsing after someone they weren't even sure was there?

Off to High School and Playing Football

When the years at St. Mary's ended, a decision had to be made about which high school I'd attend. Was I going to continue on in the Catholic school system and go to Loretto, or should I make a switch and enroll in Sault High Public School? Unlike being enrolled in St. Mary's by my parents, they said choosing the high school I would attend would be my decision to make. I didn't have to think about it much since all my friends at St. Mary's were going to Loretto; it got the nod pretty quickly.

Making the jump to high school meant freshmen would be meeting a bunch of new people for the first time. For those of us that played football, we didn't have to wait for school to start to meet one another as the preseason practices began about two weeks before school started. Loretto had a small enrollment, so the football teams were small in numbers too. Because of this, everyone from the seniors on down through the most inexperienced freshmen practiced together. In order to have enough players to conduct a proper practice, this was a necessity. You could say the freshmen didn't have a chance to "go from the frying pan into the fire" because they were thrown into the "fire" right from the start. With the practices being done that way, you got to know everyone pretty fast, and that's how the relationship with Pat and Ed Murphy, Jim Sherry, Jack and Jim Spuhler, and Joe O'Connor began. Little did we know at that time, it was the start of lifelong friendships. Regrettably, Pat and Joe are no longer with us, leaving this world way too early in life. With their absence, there are voids that can't be filled, but there are memories that can't be taken away either.

As to having successful teams, logical thinking would say we were at a disadvantage with our smaller number of players. But in my mind, just the opposite was true, and the records of those years showed it. Practicing with the veterans from the beginning developed players who were a bit smarter and tougher; when it was their time to step in, they were better prepared, and more importantly, it made for a tighter-knit group both on and off the field.

I won't bore you with a bunch of records or statistics, but I have to tell you about the 1963 football season. It definitely was the highlight season of those years at Loretto. Because it was a perfect season, we won every one of our games. Back then, high school football teams in Michigan were limited to playing eight games. After the eight games were played, your season was over as a championship playoff system wasn't in place yet, and there wouldn't be one for quite a few years. Normally, I don't like to speculate on anything, but in this case, I'll make an exception. If there was a playoff system that year, I believe we would have won it. That team was that good!

But hold on! I am proud to say that season was made even more special by Sault High's team. They had a perfect record too! To my understanding, according to the records for Michigan High School football, that was the first time two schools from the same city had perfect seasons in the same year. And it's a record that hasn't been duplicated since.

Fun at the Cabin

Having a family cabin about fifteen miles downriver from town saw me spending my summer months there. My dad would drive back and forth to work in town every day, while the rest of the family stayed there, so I missed out on most of the things my friends did in town during the summer months. But while at the cabin, I had my summer friends that included the Byes, Dunaways, Petermans, Reinharts, and Barras, along with Bob Perkins, a good friend who also went to Loretto. We had bonfires, went fishing and such, but most of the time, we could be found on the beach or swimming in the waters of the St. Mary's River. Becoming such good friends, nobody wanted to see those summers end and have to part ways until next summer. When it came close to the end of the school year, I was itching to get back there. It was like living two different lives, and I'm grateful I was able to do so; they were friendships to be cherished and times to be remembered.

It rarely happened, but every so often, I'd end up back in town for a night or two during the summer, so I had to find out if anything was happening. Well, guess what? It seemed like most of the time, a few of the guys had planned on heading to the river to go swimming. That was OK with me. I loved to swim, and that's what I probably would have been doing at the cabin anyhow. There was a difference, though; in town, instead of beaches, the riverbank was lined with various marine- related businesses, so the swimming holes were off the docks and in the slips of these places. I remember, the first time they brought me there, I wasn't too sure of it; I thought we'd just get kicked out. But that wasn't the case; none of the people working there ever said a word. It was like we weren't even there to them. It was, as I found out, a really good place to swim; the heights of the docks and depths of the water were perfect for diving, and the water in the slips always seemed to be a bit warmer than the river itself. I wasn't there a lot but always enjoyed it when I was. What a difference time makes. Can you imagine any business allowing kids to do anything like that on their property in today's world?

Friends for Life

The molding of our different personalities that began on the football field led to new ideas and exploits, some of which were a bit off the wall, to put it mildly—so much so that "Moose" Swart, a very popular volunteer assistant coach, after hearing about some stuff we pulled, made the comment "You're a crazy bunch!" You know, he might have been right, but we always had fun, and by the grace of God, we made it through everything unscathed.

As I look back, I can't deny we might have been "a crazy bunch" as "Moose" Swart said, but there isn't a bunch I would rather have gone through those years with. Even though many years have gone by and there are many miles between most of us, the friendships are still alive and strong.

My sister Lori has a little plaque in her kitchen that pretty much says it all. The message is this:

"Friends are family you choose."

16. The Summer Fun at Sherman Park

Sherman Park opened on Labor Day in 1931 and was named after Henry Sherman, one of the longtime city managers of the Sault. Sherman Park was the place for family outings, picnics, and reunions. It became the place where all the Sault kids wanted to go on a hot summer day. If they didn't have a pool, kids found their way to the park. Sherman Park was a sixty-eight-acre park located on the upper St. Mary's River and was the city's only public beach. It was a great beach too. It was located in the Algonquin region of our town. We had a campground and a playground there with a large picnic area with picnic tables, horseshoe pits, and restrooms. In the 1950s, there was even a small wildlife park there too. I'm sure it's improved much more since then, but it was a pretty cool place to go, and everyone seemed to go there. The water was always very nice, and you could see the ships passing in the river channel moving up through Lake Superior. We always liked to catch the ships' waves and surf them as they moved in toward shore.

Our family used to go there often when we didn't have time to go to the Pines out by Bay Mills, and we would still have a little picnic. The water made the difference; it was shallow until you walked out deep enough by the raft, but it was always warm, not freezing cold, like our beautiful Lake Superior. Kids of all ages were there playing ball, playing on the swings and slides, yelling and screaming, and just having a grand time having fun. A lot of kids from the Sault learned how to swim there as most of my family did. Let me tell you, that water at Sherman Park would spoil you. It was that nice and warm, and it was still very refreshing. It didn't have the gorgeous waves of our large lake, so we could learn how to swim without be swallowed up by those large waves that Superior was known for. But after visiting there three to four, trying different swimming patterns and swim strokes, we all would say "Let's go back to the Pines" as we all thought we could swim much stronger and better now.

17. "Say, Kids, It's Howdy Doody Time"

One of the most popular children's shows on television during the 1950s was Howdy Doody, starring Buffalo Bob and, of course, Howdy. It was a children's television show, and all the kids loved it. My family sure did. Howdy Doody, of course, was the star of the show. He was a redheaded marionette created, operated, and voiced by Bob Smith from Buffalo, New York, a popular radio personality and a singer! He always went by Buffalo Bob.

As the show and character grew in popularity, so too did his commercial appeal. All our local stores in the Soo, like S. S. Kresge's, Scotts, and Woolworths, were carrying the merchandise from the television show. I just remember the four main characters, and I know there were others. There was Howdy Doody, Buffalo Bob, Clarabell the Clown, and his sister Heidi Doody. They lived in a fictional town called Doodyville, and every Saturday morning, for thirty minutes, the show would be on.

A live audience of young kids my age made the show fun and exciting. Howdy was pure Americana; he had plenty of freckles, but we kids all knew he just had forty-eight freckles totaling the number of states in our country, and in the fifties, we just had the forty-eight states. It was kids in the live audience that sang the song and started the show. Do you remember the tune and the fun you had singing the song? What a song! We would all join in at home.

It's Howdy Doody time.
It's Howdy Doody time.
Bob Smith and Howdy too
Say "Howdy do" to you.
Let's give a rousing cheer
'Cause Howdy Doody's here.
It's time to start the show,
So, kids, let's go!

18. The Lone Ranger on Our Radio

I was one of the kids who really loved listening to the radio show The Lone Ranger. We all did really as we didn't have a television then. When we moved to the big house on Cedar Street in 1955, we finally purchased a television and began watching the TV series. So we listened to a lot of radio. Every one of us had our own special show we listened to. Mine was the masked man called Keemo Sabe and his sidekick, Tonto. My sister Mary would listen to it with me all the time. We often talked about moving out to the Old West and buying our own ranch. We all liked Tonto as he was a Mohawk Indian from Ontario.

At the very beginning of the radio show, an announcer introduced each episode with the following:

> In the early days of the western United States, a masked man and an Indian rode the plains, searching for truth and justice. Return with us now to those thrilling days of yesteryear, when from out of the past come the thundering hoofbeats of the great horse Silver! The Lone Ranger rides again!

It was a pretty simple script really. At the beginning of each episode, the magnificent white stallion, Silver, would rear up with the Lone Ranger on his back, then off they would go, with the ranger shouting out, "Hi-yo, Silver!" Tonto could occasionally be heard to urge on his mount by calling out, "Gettem up, Scout!" At the end of each episode, with the mission completed, one of the radio characters would always ask the sheriff or other authority, "Who was that masked man?" And when it was explained, "Oh, he's the Lone Ranger!" The ranger and Tonto would be heard galloping off on Scout and Silver, with the cry "Hi-Yo, Silver, away!"

19. Neighborhood Stores Cover the Soo

Growing up in the Soo back in the fifties, it didn't take me long to sort out the five major pillars to Soo life; its lifeblood. They were our industry, our hockey, our churches, our schools, and our neighborhood stores. So what did the family names of Andary, Bagnall, Byer, Bye, Best, Bosbous, Brown, Calery, Cannelo, Cook, Dalimonte, DeMolen, Doran, Dorgan, Ermatinger, Falco, France, Hare, Haller, Ranta, LaBerto, Perry, Callaghan, O'Connor, Jarvie, LeLievre, Matheson, McKinney, Napoleon, Neville, Nelson, Perry, Wydra, Pacquin, Pingatore, Potvin, Quinn, Sinigos, Tobias, Vaukonen, and Venious all have in common? They all had neighborhood stores in our town. We had over sixty of them back then, and they were spotted throughout every region of our town.

They became a very important part of our life. They fed us and were always there for us. Don't you remember running to the store to get some eggs or milk or bread and charging it to your family account or quickly getting a pound of hamburger for your dinner? Sure, we had the big stores, and back then, it was the Red Owl, Piggly Wiggly, the A&P Store, and the Soo Co-op. But the very lifeblood of the Soo was our local neighborhood stores. They were always family owned and operated. We knew them well, and they knew us. They were centers of activity in our regions of the town and helped give the town its energy and life. It was always busy around them. They became our anchors, really.

Some of them had butcher shops, so you could always pick up your fresh meat. If your mom wanted a good cut of roast or a nice fillet, she would know whom to speak with to get it. It was all very personal. All of them covered the basics—bread, eggs, and milk—but some really did a bang-up job selling beer, wine, and newspapers, even cigars. Some were great candy stores, and some had the best ethnic food ever. More important than anything else, though, is, we knew them. We knew their families and grew up with their kids. In the East End, we had four stores, and if you included parts of Riverside Drive and part of Shunk Road, we had seven, and we went to them all. It made growing up easy and fun having them.

The Ermatinger Store on E. Portage Street and the Hare Store on East Spruce Street were our favorites. Both of them were located just around the corner and a few blocks from where we lived. The Ermatinger Store had some special significance, however. It was owned by ole Mike Ermatinger. He was a very dear friend of my father. Dad was his banker and his fishing buddy. The Ermatinger family had been in the Soo for many generations. Their neighborhood store was located on the corner of Portage and Sova Streets, directly across the Union Carbide. It had been there since the early 1930s, and as I said, it was just about two blocks from where we lived. Mike had a son, Bob, who grew up in the business. He was the trained butcher. We got our fresh meats from there. We all liked Bob, and really, he ran the neighborhood store as Mike aged. But Mike was always there into the early evening as that was when his old friends from the Carbide and neighborhood would come over for a visit. They all would gather and share a beer downstairs in the store's basement with him.

In the summertime, Dad would always take me with him to go to the store to visit Mike. About 7:00 p.m., we would walk down to the store. I remember all the names of the men—and see their faces still—who always gathered there. From the Carbide, there was Ollie and Reino. Ollie was a big Swede with a thick accent. He was a neighbor of Mike's. Reino was a real Finlander, and he was always laughing and had the funniest stories. Then there was Chucky. He always arrived with a very loud hello; he was an Indian, but today, we more politely call him a Native American. He spoke so fast. He was hard for me to follow, but all the men nodded their heads when he spoke. So I thought they must have understood him. Dutch too was there, but he always came in late. He was our Bluebird bread man. He and Mike were good friends too. Dad didn't know him well, but all the boys of our neighborhood knew our Bluebird Bakery man. Bob would close the store about 9:00 p.m., and he would come downstairs and join all the men.

By that time, though, all the men had a few too many. Bob knew that Mike was not supposed to be drinking at all but let him enjoy himself, if he watched himself. Mike would always say when Bob started chewing at him, "Now that you're here, son, I'll watch myself." So we all knew that was the magic word to begin to close down the evening's visit and get home. The store stayed in the family until the early sixties. Mike had died, and Bob ran everything and had a young family. He eventually sold the store to Hank DeMolen, a successful store operator from the west end of town. Hank too ran a great operation. He was friendly, always jovial, and helpful to his customers. He became deeply loved by our East Enders. We all thought he was just like ole Mike.

20. My Uncle Dongol's Fingers

My favorite uncle and aunt was Dongol and Doine McDonald, on my dad's side of the family. Now that's not saying I didn't love my mother's oldest sister, Aunt Vera, because I truly did; she was the best cook ever. And my mother had two special brothers she always liked a great deal. Glenn was her older brother, and Fred was the baby of the family—all of us loved them. But it was still Dongol and Doine. They were the McDonalds.

How they got their names was interesting. Their real names were Donald and Geraldine McDonald, and their children were our closest cousins: Joannie, Danny, and Ruthie.

Now Doine's name was easy; it came from our father. As the story went, when he was a little boy, he used to call her Doine as he could not say her real name of Geraldine. That name stuck when we all were kids, and as adults, it remained. Dongol was a little different as he already had a nickname of Dusty. He was a very good ballplayer when he was a young man. He tried out for the old St. Louis Cardinals as a third baseman. He always would drive to the base headfirst; thus, they all called him Dusty. Both my parents called him Donald and Dusty. When my brother John was a little boy, he couldn't pronounce Uncle Donald. So he came up with the name of Dongol, and that stuck with all of us from our early childhood years to our adult lives. He was called Dongol, and he was ours, and Doine was too.

He was always special to me. He always talked to me and teased me. He always showed me how to spit, especially into the big spittoon he had on the living-room floor in front of the television, next to his reclining chair. I remember several things about him—his big smile, his huge hands, and how he picked me up and held me by my feet upside down. But the one thing that I will always remember was his fingers. He used to twirl them and roll them and then stick one out in front of me for me to copy. Of course, at that young age, I did not know which finger I was pointing out back to him. I just did it and snarled my teeth as he did to me. But I did enjoy him as he was funny and very warm indeed. So while John and Dan were playing and Mary and Ruthie and sometimes Joannie were playing, I was playing with Dongol, not knowing what trouble he would cause for me later with his fingers.

The families often gathered for Sunday mass at St. Isaac Jogues Catholic Church. It was a Jesuit mission church set up to help the Native American community of our Shunk Road area of town. The parish priest we all loved was Fr. Prudhomme. He was a French Jesuit priest who came to us from the Indian Ontario parish of Batchawanna Bay along the shore of northern Lake Superior. He was a white-haired older man but very saintly. He had a nicely trimmed white beard and spoke with a broken French accent. But we all understood his English. Although we belonged to St. Mary's Parish and the McDonalds belonged to St. Joseph's Parish, the Jesuits always held a deep bond with the McCarthy family and still do to this day.

But here at this lovely little mission church—with a saintly priest like Fr. Prudhomme conducting mass—is where my uncle's teachings and his fingers got me in deep trouble.

The McDonald family was sitting in the pew ahead of us, all of them. The McCarthys then marched in and knelt right behind them. We said our hellos, and then mass started. Dongol was right in front of me, and we were playing silly little games when we should have been listening to the priest and praying. He then stuck his finger out to me, but no one saw him doing it. He kept it up and kept it up until Doine stopped him. I laughed out loud as he was caught. I knew Doine would chew him out. She didn't want me getting into trouble.

So things quieted down for a few minutes until it was time for Father to speak to those attending mass; it was called his homily. As Dongol was sitting down, he turned around and winked at me. I held up my middle finger and put it in front of his face, so not only could he see it, but the entire congregation could see me giving the finger to my uncle. Now I thought it deserved a smile or a laugh, but my mother grabbed me by my left ear and took me out of the church so quick. I don't even recall touching those eighteen stairs it took to walk out of the church. I just remember, as clear now as it happened then, how I embarrassed her. I probably got a belt or two, but I knew my ear was very sore.

This story has lived on in our family for sixty years. It has brought great laughter to all of us and still does to the next generation. Dongol and I never did it again, but I always liked playing with my Uncle Dongol. He was very special. He was a great troublemaker for me, but I deeply and truly loved him. No doubt, I teased him as much as he teased me. Even as I aged and would gather in the McDonald kitchen, I would always get with Dongol and enjoy a joke, a laugh and just have a nice chat. He was a true and proud Scotsman. My uncle had huge hands, a huge heart, and a lovely, warm smile that I will always remember.

A Tribute to Dongol

Oh Flower of Scotland, when will we see
Your likes again.
That fought and died for, your wee bit Hill and Glen,
And stood against him, proud Edward's Army,
And sent him homeward, to think again.

Those days are past now, and in the past They must remain.
But we can still rise now, and be the nation again.

(Roy Williamson, "Flower of Scotland," Scotland's
national anthem)

21. "Oh no, Mike Has the Croup"

It seems, growing up, our family could always count on us kids getting head colds and bad coughs, sometimes bronchitis, sometimes pneumonia, and even the famous croup. My cousin Dan McDonald suffered from asthmatic attacks all throughout his childhood and into his teenage years, while I myself suffered at six months old, five years old, and eight years old. I had pneumonia. It's funny, really, because back then, they treated you in a hospital for two weeks. The best part was missing all that school, but the worst part other than those three shots in the butt you got each day was the making up of homework I had to do.

Once the winter started, my brother John would always get head colds, as would my sister Kathleen, while my sister Mary shared the bronchitis jinx with me. She would get it first, it seemed, and passed it on to me, her little brother.

But the one thing I got every winter, and there was no vaccine for, was a horrible cough we called the croup. It was much like a whooping cough, almost, but this was different. This was a barky, raspy cough that sounded like a seal asking for his next meal. It started always with me without warning. As a child, I would suddenly sit up in bed with a barking cough, and I mean a deep barking cough. When you first hear it, you get a little scared as your airwaves are pretty blocked up and it's hard to breathe, but then you cough. It was loud and would wake the entire house. It can be frightening, and at first, I was surely scared. After a while, I just needed to make sure it didn't lead to pneumonia because I hated the treatment at the hospital. Sure, the nurses and doctors were nice, but I hated those shots and didn't want to ever go back there again. We always treated it with moist air from a humidifier. But first, Mother would put my head over a boiling pot of water in a bowl and cover my head with a towel. She said this would open the airwaves, and surely, she was right. Then out came the Vicks, and she would rub it throughout my entire chest area and then cover it. My mom was pretty good at stuff like that because our grandmother was a nurse, and she really had some old-fashioned remedies. Let me tell you, she really did. Once the airwaves opened, Gramma had Mom make up what we all called Gramma's mustard plasters and apply it to my chest. These wrappings of hers would take out all the infection from my chest and lungs and bronchial tubes.

My dad used to get the croup when he was a boy, and as a man, he would continue to get heavy chest colds. We all would enjoy Gramma's mustard plasters on his chest. She really loaded the dry mustard on his towels and then wrapped it on his chest. They burned and burned, but after twenty-four hours, whatever ailed you was gone. Granma knew her stuff.

We knew the croup was passed down through the generations as we called it back then. Today, it's just a DNA thing. But it is funny because today they now have a medical term called adult croup. I get it still every year. The treatments are very similar to what my mother used to do when I was a child. It was a great time for my mom and me, and she was always careful and watchful. She too didn't want me in the hospital again as well. She dreaded that darn pneumonia. But we talked for hours, it seems, around those sick times. We would play cards and sometimes play monopoly because she didn't want me jumping around getting a sweat. It seems now they were the only times we ever were alone—just her and me. It was our chance to just be together and talk, and we did. We did for hours. As I think about it now, it was she that gave me the first song I believe I ever heard and learned. She always sang it for me while I was in the hospital as visiting time was over and bedtime was near. Mothers are pretty special.

Mom's Song

The little toy dog is covered with dust
But sturdy and stanch he stands
And the little toy soldier is red with rust
And his musket moulds in his hands

Time was when the little toy dog was new
And the soldier was passing fair

And that was the time when our Little Boy Blue
Kissed them and put them there

"Now, don't you go till I come," he said,
"And don't you make any noise!"
So, toddling off to his trundle-bed
He dreamt of the pretty toys

And, as he was dreaming, an angel song
Awakened our Little Boy Blue
Oh! The years are many, the years are long
But the little toy friends are true

Ay, faithful to Little Boy Blue they stand
Each in the same old place
Awaiting the touch of a little hand
The smile of a little face

And they wonder, as waiting the long years through
In the dust of that little chair
What has become of our Little Boy Blue
Since he kissed them and put them there

(Eugene Field, "Little Boy Blue" [1894])

22. "Let's Go to the Starlite Drive-In Theater"

It was always a special treat going to the outdoor movie theater called the Starlite Drive-In. It was five miles out on old US 2 in the Pine Grove area of Soo Township and right down by Osborne Dairy, who used to deliver our milk and butter. It opened always in the late spring of the year, just on weekends, so the older kids could have something to do and somewhere to go. And you know what they used to do. But really, it got going during the summer months when school was completely out. It was a real treat for us kids driving out from town. Kids came in from the country as well, and they would enjoy it. Thinking about it now, it was probably a very pleasant way for our parents to get their kids to go to sleep. It was very rare in our family that we watched the entire movie. The movies always started at dusk or right before it was pitch-black outside. The end came shortly after midnight, and as I said, most of us were sleeping.

My parents were always good about getting us drinks, and each of us had some popcorn. We would all bundle up in our blankets and wait for the movie to start. There was always time for playful activities with the four of us. We were pretty good about not fighting and causing trouble, especially between Mary and me. My dad would always try to park our car right in the middle of the outdoor parking lot. It seemed we were always right in front of this large theater screen. We had a perfect view. He would then put the speaker on our window and roll the window up snug so the cool night air would not freeze us. The place was always jam- packed with cars. Kids were everywhere. The sounds of them playing and running around and screaming were all acceptable behavior by all the parents until the lights started flashing—this was our signal the movie was going to start. We knew we better head back to our cars and snuggle back into our blankets for the start of the movie.

Here we were—the six of us. Kathy was just a baby, but we squeezed nicely in our parents' car, watching a movie and staying as quiet as could be. Now tell me that wasn't like heaven for our mother and father raising four little kids. To this very day, I have the fondest of memories when I think of the Starlite Drive-In.

23. My Heroes Have Always Been Cowboys

As a young boy growing up in the fifties, most of us had one war hero, one hockey hero, or at least one cowboy we liked. I happened to like three men. The first, of course, had to be the Lone Ranger. He was something special, I always thought. His horse, Silver, was very special too. Next, it had to be Audie Murphy, a decorated WWII hero. He was such a good and kind man and just an overall very nice, likable guy but also a movie star. Then it had to be Terry Sawchuk. He was the greatest goalie ever—with a big, big smile and a face that a lawn mower seemed to have driven over.

I enjoyed watching them on our television as much as I could and on the big theater screen if they were starring in a movie or even going to the Pullar with my dad to see Terry Sawchuk and the Red Wings practice and play. They were all great characters, and they always inspired me. They each had a real defined strength.

Growing up, I used these traits to identify my own boyhood heroes. Young men and boys a little older than me who were kind and fair were happy more than sad and yet were scrappy in their own way to defend what they thought was right. My boyhood heroes were an important part of my life growing up in our East End.

These folks may surprise people who knew me. But maybe not. The first was my big brother, John. He always was and will always be my big brother. He was a gentle giant, kind, always honest (he really couldn't lie his way out of a thing), and very stern at times but very fair. Sure, he drove me crazy at times as he was such a goody-two-shoes type of kid. He never raised a hand to me or hit me. Yeah, he teased me a bit and enjoyed, I think, me losing my temper. He was also the first one to get me out of trouble. He was graceful at every sport he played—an excellent skater and passer, always playing with a huge smile, always wanting to be helpful. John was a happy kid. He was a good big brother. I always looked up to him.

The second was my cousin Danny McDonald. Danny was funny, always laughing at anything. He was very competitive with everything he did because he was so small. I was three years younger than Dan. He always passed his good clothes down to me as he was just a few inches taller than me. I too was a blond-headed tiny kid like him. Some thought we were brothers. We acted the same in so many ways. What I loved about him, though, was, he was fearless. He was the toughest little kid on his block, literally. Where John was probably the best stickhandler I ever saw play hockey, Danny had to be the fastest I ever saw skate. And he didn't care a hoot how big the other players were; he always challenged them.

The last of my boyhood heroes was my neighbor Tim Kinney. Tim was always, and still is today, a very gentle giant with a child's heart. He was protective to those he liked and always was extremely careful—because of his size and height— so he wouldn't hurt us. So when we all played any big sport, he could only play using one hand, and we would tie the other hand behind his back just so things would be fair. Yet he was just one year older than most of us. He too was just a kid. So many times, the kids in our neighborhood forgot that about him because he was so big. He never complained a bit, and his graciousness and kindness to a small guy like myself made him very special to me. I really appreciated him. He was fun to be around. Being with him, you knew you were safe.

Also, I need to add an honorable mention here, my older cousin Mike Wieneke. He was a cousin on the Irish side of our family, the Hassetts. But he was a kind and happy older cousin. He was always getting me out of fights. He lived on Sova Street, around the corner from us on Cedar Street. His younger brother Pat and I were together always, it seemed, throughout our grade school years. During the summer daylight hours, Mike was always with us or near us. He really loved my mom and dad, and he became our adopted brother although he was just a cousin. He was a real good guy.

It is sort of funny in a way, isn't it? Even as you age, those traits are still important today. I was very fortunate to have my heroes with me through most of my life. All four of them were real characters when they were young and kept that same trait as they became older. But having them made life a lot easier. I love them more today.

24. Going to the Memorial Gardens for a Hockey Game

We used to enjoy going to the memorial gardens in Soo, Ontario, to watch a Greyhounds hockey game. Of course, we had to take the ferryboat, and that always made it more fun. The gardens were quite a facility. It was much newer than the Pullar Stadium in Sault, Michigan, and a little bigger. The neatest thing I thought was, it was located right on Queen Street. It was right in the middle of the city.

About four thousand people could be seated there, and every Greyhound game seemed to be standing room only. That's the way it was when they played our own Soo Indians anyway. The seats were all wooden benches, and I remember them being painted light blue. The gardens had more rows of seats at the ends of the arena than along the sides. So the inside was much different from the Pullar, but the hockey crowds were not. These folks loved their hockey; they ate it, they loved it, and they slept it. The gardens' most distinctive feature was their memorial tower and red-lighted beacon. The beacon was always lit on nights the Greyhounds were playing, so driving up to the stadium, the first thing you would see was the lit beacon. It always captured my attention, and it was always pretty cool. Dad explained that the importance of the memorial was to honor Soo Canada's military who lost their lives during WWII.

Our own Soo Indians played in the Northern Ontario Hockey Association, the Senior League, and our greatest rivalry was with the Soo Greyhounds. So anytime Dad was free, he would take my brother and me to go see them play, whether it was at the Pullar or in Soo, Ontario. The league back then had some great teams and great players. Two of the other teams I recall clearly were the Sudbury

Wolves and the North Bay Trappers. I always marveled at our nicknames of the teams, the Greyhounds, Wolves, Trappers, and our own Indians. In 1955, we had our best record ever for our Soo Indians hockey team, and our hero was Laurie Peterson. He was, by far, the very best player in the league. At least that was the talk from the men when they gathered in the smoking rooms after each period. The hockey, as I said before, was semiprofessional. These boys got paid, and they were fast. They were also tough, and they seemed to shoot the puck harder than I ever saw shot before.

But the sounds at the gardens were greater and deeper than ours at the Pullar. They had horns and huge drums that would be blowing and pounding and clanging throughout the entire game. People, of course, would be yelling, and that was typical, and players would be fighting, and we did that. But the sound was so strong we could not hear one another talk. That was common for the memorial gardens, and I was there plenty of times. That's what always made it so very exciting, I thought. I loved their brand of hockey. They loved playing for their fans as our boys, the Soo Indians, did. It was great hockey in the fifties.

Final Chapter of Sounds

25. The Greatest Sound I Ever Heard in the Soo

Ask this question to the people in the Soo, "What is the greatest sound you have ever heard?" I'm sure everyone who answers the question will stand by their answer. But some animal lovers will say the call of a wolf pack you could hear in Northern Ontario or the roar of a hungry black bear in the spring or the serene, lonely sound of a loon or the sounds of a flock of geese or even our own seagulls along our St. Mary's River. Motor enthusiasts no doubt would say the sound coming from the cobra pipes of a Harley motorcycle, the revving up of engines beginning the I-500 Snowmobile Race, or the Air Force Thunderbirds jet team that would practice at our old Kincheloe AFB. Some will want to talk about the great performances and plays held at the Ritchie Auditorium in the old Soo High School, the beautiful and artistic sounds from the choral presentations of the Mary Wood Choir, the drums and bugles of our boys from WWI, or any other choir such as Sault Canada's community choir and their beautiful rendition of singing "O Canada." But give to me the spirit and passion and sound of one little man with a heart of gold to rally the Soo and its neighboring communities and its sports teams. His sound was more than special. It was the greatest. In the late 1950s until the mid 1980s, he was our community and regional cheerleader. His name was Felix "Buttsy" Tavern.

Many knew him simply as Buttsy. I first met him as a young boy in the East End. Mr. Tavern, as I called him, was our meterman. He worked for the Edison Sault Electric Company. He would visit our home on Cedar Street, and if he saw us outside, he would chat for a while before going to the next house and meter. He was making sure our billing was correct and our electric use was in line with our billing. Our mother always enjoyed a chat with him; everyone did. He was very friendly and warm and always smiling. If his job was customer relations, he put a good face to the Edison Soo name. He was very well received by my neighbors and deeply liked by all.

On weekends, at most basketball, football, and hockey games, he really became Buttsy. He would dress up wearing the school sweater, and there were several schools throughout the region that gave him their varsity sweater. But at halftime of any game, he would start his community cheer. He would run out onto the middle of the floor and call the community together. We needed to support the team. He was there to lead us in cheers. Oftentimes, he would wear the Soo's varsity letter on one side and the competing school's letter from a different community on the other. He would cheer for both teams. His clap was very loud, and it made a loud pop as the palms of his hands were clapped together. I can hear his voice today: "Come on, Sault Sainte Marie. Come on, Brimley. Come on, Newberry. Let's give these kids a cheer of support." People enjoyed him and would follow his lead. They loved his spirit and passion. He embodied the love for the Sault Sainte Marie community and the entire region we all had and felt privately, but he put his on display. We all loved him and admired how he supported our local teams. The parents, especially those who had children on those teams, appreciated Buttsy. Buttsy didn't have children playing; he just had a heart of gold. Somehow, we know we'll never see his likes again. Buttsy was always Uncle Sam at local parades and did all this until he was eighty-two. He passed at the age of eighty-five. But he'll be remembered, not only for his unique sound, but also for everything he did for his hometown. His was the greatest sound I have ever heard.

> The purpose of life is not to be happy. It is to be useful,
>
> To be honorable,
>
> To be compassionate,
>
> To have it make some difference That you have lived
> and lived well.
>
> —Ralph Waldo Emerson

The Smells of My Childhood

The sense of smell is developed at a very young age, and in fact, it is said that children have a better sense of smell than their parents or grandparents. As I said earlier in my first book, The Sounds and Smell of My Childhood, the Soo, with our beautiful St. Mary's River, produced the most interesting smells and aromas.

One of the things you find out as you age is that the sense of smell has different levels for different people, and in some people, the sense of smell is very well-developed early in life. It fills our brains with memories and often triggers social responses, allowing us to recall things from our past we felt were hidden for decades.

Have you ever noticed how a certain smell can remind you of old memories? For instance, every Christmas, our father would always go across to Canada on the ferryboat and buy a Christmas gift for our mother, a bottle of White Shoulders perfume. She loved wearing it. The smell of that perfume today reminds me of her. Or the smell of a homemade apple pie cooking in a home or a bakery—how that reminds me of sitting in Ma's kitchen as a little boy at the farm, helping her cook one of her delicious apple pies. And the smell of dirty socks reminds me still of my big brother, and the smell of scented candles burning reminds me of my altar-boy days serving benediction with my brother as well.

Each one of us has in our nose "the smell device." Did you know we can distinguish ten thousand different smells? Growing up in the Soo and living along our beautiful river, I developed my sense of smell early in life. I had to, just like my older brother, John, developed his. How about yourself? Can you recall your youth? Do you remember the smells of your childhood? Here are some more of mine.

First Chapter of the Smells

1. Driving through the Pines to Lake Superior

It was always fun going as a family for a summer drive through the pine trees to Lake Superior for our Sunday picnic. The Pines, as they were called, were located just west of the Bay Mills Indian Reservation. It was a pleasant, picturesque drive, and once we passed the Chippewa Indian burial grounds and the historic lighthouse, we knew we were getting close.

It was always interesting and fun to stop at both of these historic places on our return home. We took plenty of time, really, and did our own tour of these sites. In the summertime, you would see artists, photographers, and all kinds of history nuts doing their part for preservation.

The Iroquois Point Lighthouse was a special place, and artists from all over—literally everywhere—tried to capture its beauty. The artists were of all ages, but one always caught my eye. He always seemed to be there when we were. He was a very elderly man and had to be an elder of the tribe, I thought. My dad said he was as he knew him. His name was Mr. Cameron. He enjoyed visiting with the kids more than the adults. He didn't have, like so many other artists had, any fancy paints or fancy boards. His paints looked old, and the canvas he painted on looked older. But how he used to swing his brush and talk to himself while he painted always amazed me. I thought that was different. His paintings looked different too. It almost seemed there was someone inside him talking to him, telling him to use this color or that color. He was always mumbling to himself. Yes, he was different.

I knew a painter in my younger days,
A man, who lived with brushes, sticks and stones.
His days were filled with canvas scenes

Of browns and blues and meadow greens. And the world just
passed on by his door. He lived, but lived alone.

But he could paint a picture, And he could capture life,
And no one ever felt things more than he.
He was never much for roses,
He'd sooner paint the thorns.
Cause he found a keener beauty there,
That no one else could see.

And long through the night, a faded yellow light,
Would burn inside the room where he would stand.
And play the old victrola and drink his rusty wine.And
conduct the Mozart music with his heart and shaking hand.

(David Mallett, "Phil Brown")

The pines, with their sweet scent, began at the lighthouse, and for several miles
to the lake, we enjoyed that great aroma. Our brother John always maintained
that, and no one doubted him on issues like this. We drove all the way on an
old gravel road in the 1950s, but the Pines were just that—huge pine trees
that bordered the lakeshore road, and unless you knew differently, they really
protected the very pristine parts of Lake Superior from tourists, other picnic
dwellers, barbecue enthusiasts, and screaming children. No one went there other
than our family, or so we thought. We wanted it to become our own private
place, and anytime a visitor came nearby, we would move up the beach to be
totally private. We often asked our parents why we couldn't buy it so it could
be just ours. Lake Superior was a magnificent lake; it was a clear, clean, cold
body of water. It was the deepest of our Great Lakes, and like the St. Mary's

River, we felt bound by it. We all loved the lake; it's like it belonged to each of us. It was ours.

But the Pines had the greatest and sweetest smell—a scent that time wouldn't let you forget. We all looked forward to being in that wonderful zone. It lasted as long as we were there. It just wasn't a passing wind or breeze; it was a beautiful aroma, and we lived in it. It was truly special. I'm sure that each of my siblings felt something special being a part of this; for me, it was as if I were floating in it—a sense of being free.

Once we landed and parked our car deep in the Pines but off the road so the car couldn't be seen, we walked the one hundred yards or so to a pristine and untouched beach. Our mother then set up our picnic.

Kids being kids, the first thing we did, of course, was to challenge ourselves. The first sibling to jump into the cold, clear water by diving right into it headfirst would be the winner. Most of the time, my brother John and I won. But after a while, it didn't matter who won or who gave the loudest yell or scream. Each of us did. The water was very cold. The body would turn its own shade of purple if we stayed in the lake too long. Mother would tell us it was time to get out of the water. Once the color of our lips started to turn to a purplish blue, we didn't argue with her, and we shivered for a good twenty minutes warming up. Even our father would finally loosen up and take his shirt off and run barefoot in the sand. He would only get his toes wet, but he wouldn't go in.

The second thing we did as kids was to pick those delicious wild blueberries located throughout the pine forests. They had a great taste, and that flavor lasted for hours. These were very small blueberries. They were much different from the large ones you would buy in a supermarket. In fact, they were tiny. But my gosh, they were so tasty. We would always pick enough for our picnic lunch but also enough for our mother to bake a small blueberry tart when we got home. And she would. It was special and delicious.

The third thing we had to do was to get some wood—sticks and even dried driftwood—to have a small fire so we could then sit down and enjoy the picnic Mother had assembled. The fire kept everyone warm and kept those little black flies we called No See Ums away. Mother always did a bang-up job for our picnics. She always had her homemade potato salad, and my father just loved it. We all did. Then she would make different kinds of sandwiches for each of us, like peanut butter and jam, cheese, lettuce, and tomato, and my brother John's special peanut-butter-and-pickle sandwich. We brought some pop to drink, and all was well with a wonderful day. We talked and laughed and didn't want the day to end. We all knew Monday started the new week.

2. Saturday Matinee at the Soo Theatre

Going to a double feature for the Saturday matinee at the Soo Theatre was hugely popular with all the kids of our town. The theater was built in 1930, and for all those years, it was a center point of entertainment, especially for the kids of the community. Our community leaders were pretty good to us kids back then. We had several places to play and just have fun. The various ball fields, Kaine's Rink, the Pullar Stadium, the Sherman Park Beach, and our own Soo Theatre were always busy with kids. This, of course, was before skateboarding parks became popular or bike paths were built along our major streets and long before climbing walls were erected. Going downtown to a movie was always fun and exciting. But there was always a long—no, no, not just long, but a very long, long line going right back to the bridge on Ashmun Street. Everyone tried to get there at least an hour early so they could get their ticket and a seat. The 1:00 p.m. doubleheader would last until 5:00 p.m. Most of the time, your stomach would be filled up with candy, popcorn, and lots of pop. That was always our first stop before we took a seat, and the smell of buttered popcorn ran throughout the theater.

I was not allowed to go to the movies on my own or with my friends until I was ten years old. I would normally go with my cousin Pat. My big brother, John, had to take us with his friends. They were teenagers. John was always pretty good about it, and he was always watchful of me so I wouldn't get into any trouble. Even at that young age, trouble seemed to follow me, as our dad would say, so John had a double role. He needed to take Pat and me to the theater with his friends. Worst of all, he thought he needed to be a babysitter, which he did not like. As I said, he was pretty good about it, but like the nuns and priests, he too had rules that I had to follow or he wouldn't take me again. Pat had an older brother, Mike, whom we all liked, but he wanted no part of taking us to a movie. So I did try to stay at my very best with John because going downtown for a Saturday afternoon was very special. I was just an East End boy, and going to a movie took me out of the neighborhood.

I remember going to my first double feature; it was an Abbott and Costello movie and The Blob. The first movie was very funny as those fellows were hilarious, and to this day, they still make me laugh. But the second scared the bejabbers out of me. A meteor had fallen from the sky and landed on the earth. A young couple then goes to check it out to see what it was. They open up the meteor, and out comes this little jellylike creature. It then starts consuming everything it touches—everything. The sounds of the boys yelling and all the girls screaming made the darn movie even scarier, I thought. The worst scene was when the blob oozes into a local theater, just like ours, and consumes the projectionist and then starts to consume some of the audience. Fortunately, I thought it was just some members of the audience. The rest of the audience runs out screaming from the theater. Our audience was screaming too, and it was really very loud. Thank goodness no one ran out, or it would have caused an immediate flight out of our theater.

It had a strange ending, I remember. Kids and teenagers all have guns, and they, the police, and the military are used to freeze the blob. They ship it off to the Arctic and let it parachute down on the ice. That's where the blob is today. After the movie ended, we needed to hustle and get home right away for dinner.

I can't tell you the number of dreams I had of that movie and how I hoped our Arctic stays frozen. Believe me, I looked forward to getting back to the comforts of my home.

3. Being an Acolyte:
The Latin High Mass

My brother John and I were altar boys. It was the perfect role for John as, from a little boy, he was destined to be the priest in the family, while my sister Mary was sure to be the nun. When I was eight years old, John had already been an altar boy for four years, and he took me on to be his second partner with another boy called John. He was in the same grade as my brother. Each mass had three altar boys on the altar.

I knew how proud my mother and grandmother were to see their two boys together up on the altar reciting our Latin prayers. John made certain I passed all the Latin tests given by our parish priests, and at that time, there were three at St. Mary's Parish. During the fifties, there was great competition between the two largest parishes of the Soo, St. Mary's and St. Joseph's, and it was all due to the two pastors of the parishes: Fr. Monroe and Fr. O'Callaghan.

The altar boys, as we called them in the fifties, have been a part of church history since the earliest times.

From the very beginning, the duties of an acolyte or learner were strictly the domain of young males as women had no place near the altar. I understood all this, but I wanted to try to get my sister Mary to replace me, and after two private conversations with John and his partner and another with one of our priests, I was told it couldn't be done. So I waited for a better chance to speak directly with the pastor, Fr. Monroe. To me, it was simple arithmetic, I thought: Mary was deeply devoted; I was not, and she should be better up on the altar than myself, I felt. So I waited.

In church history, it was a fact that we were one of the seven levels of ordained ministry in the Latin rite that culminated with deacon and, finally, priest. I had no interest in becoming a priest, but I knew it was important for my mother and grandmother. But they knew full well, priesthood and I did not mix. Besides, my brother John wanted me on his team, and he was my big brother.

Into the sixties and prior to Vatican II and its reforms, which changed the language of the mass from Latin to English, the role of altar boy became a solemn duty of dedicated youth to serve before the altar of God before reaching adulthood and marriage. I enjoyed the fact I was serving God, but I must admit some of the traditions that my brother and his partner truly loved and believed, I found hokey. The big thing was, our duties were serious and involved lots of study—more than I wanted to give it.

I get a big kick out of kids today talking about how altar serving today is a chore. They have no idea about how things were in the 1950s and '60s—what an altar boy had to do and had to learn to serve at mass.

First, all boys who made their first communion were expected to become altar boys, and that was the case with my brother John. He became an altar boy in the third grade. The other thing was, our parents expected John to be on the altar, and when my turn came, I was expected to do the same.

On Sundays, you saw only girls with their parents in the pews. The boys always served if they attended mass.

Altar boys were expected to serve from the age of seven or eight up to the age of nineteen. In this way, each church had consistently twenty to thirty altar boys on duty. When older boys went to college or got married, new ones were always there to take their place.

All the boys wishing to be on the altar practiced the many complex duties the altar boy had to perform. But first, you had to pass your Latin test, most often given by the pastor or a parish priest. Then you learned

- how to stand with hands folded,

- how to lift the priest's chasuble at the consecration,

- how to change the missal from the Epistle (first reading) side to the Gospel side of the altar,

- how to prepare the incense and the proper way to swing the thurible (incense burner) so that the sweet smoke came out in clouds at benediction or during solemn masses,

- how to properly hold the cruets of water and wine and pour the water over the fingers of the priest, and always

- how to bow properly after performing your tasks.

Then once you were accepted, the new altar boys were given a cassock (long black garment) and a starched crisp-white surplice to wear over it. Each boy had a place to hang it and was expected to take them home frequently to be laundered and starched by their parents. God help you if Father saw you in a sloppy, dirty cassock or surplice!

Before every mass, my brother John, being the leader of our team, worked with the priest while I and the other John had to prepare the altar: light the six-foot-high candles at the main altar and remove the altar cover that covered the altar. We did this while John laid out the vestments for the chalice and helped the priest dress. Then he would hand the priest his biretta, or the little black hat that the priest would wear to the altar. Now, Father was ready to begin Mass. I would ring the altar bell, and off we walked into the church carrying our candles, trying always to look saintlike.

Then, of course, there were the duties of weddings and funerals where at least two altar boys were there, even if they had to miss school! That part was fun, so oftentimes, a little politics and positioning were played with the priests. Now these church events were pretty good because families would oftentimes pay you a tip for your efforts. Being an altar boy was like being in the army; each duty had to be performed smoothly, on time, gracefully, and with full reverence.

Then finally, there was benediction and incense. I mentioned during our training, we were given instruction on how to prepare the incense and the proper way to swing the thurible (incense burner) so that the sweet smoke came out in clouds at benediction or during solemn masses.

> The idea of Benediction is really one of the most generally popular services in the Roman Catholic Church. The Blessed Sacrament is on display ordinarily an afternoon or at an evening devotion and consists in the singing of certain hymns or litanies, or canticles before the Blessed Sacrament, which is exposed upon the altar in a monstrance and is surrounded with candles. At the end, the priest or deacon, his shoulders enveloped in a veil, take the monstrance into his hands and with it make the sign of the cross in silence over the kneeling congregation. Benediction is often employed as a conclusion to other services, e.g. Vespers and the Stations of the Cross, but it is also still more generally treated as a rite complete in itself.

Then comes the incense. My brother was a stickler with this, making certain it was done right. He had his own system that the priests liked, and it was just lighting the bits of charcoal at the right time.

Incense is a sacramental used to venerate, bless, and sanctify. Its smoke conveys a sense of mystery and awe. It is a reminder of the sweet smelling presence of our Lord. Its use adds a feeling of solemnity to the Mass. The visual imagery of the smoke and the smell reinforce the transcendence of the Mass linking Heaven with Earth, allowing us to enter into the presence of God. The smoke symbolizes the burning zeal of faith that should consume all Christians, while the fragrance symbolizes Christian virtue.

All this was the official version of incense taught to us by our church. For me, I always got sick and nauseated of that smell, and no disrespect to our Lord, but I fainted when we used this for my first time at a funeral. My brother John was so embarrassed at his little brother passing out. I knew then I wasn't long for this activity, but I did serve Mass part-time through high school. It's funny, really, as the last time I served Mass was with my two sons when they were little boys themselves. Tradition does matter, I guess.

I have never forgotten that smell of incense, and no disrespect to the teachings of our church, I remember the day I fainted.

> Tantum Ergo Sacramentum
> (Song at benediction)
>
> Tantum ergo sacrementum,
> Veneremur cernui documentum,
> Novo cedat ritui.
> Praestet fides supplementum,
> Sensuum defectui.

4. Our Bluebird Bakery Man, Dutch

It's funny how times today seem to have changed yet have stayed the same. In the 1950s, we used to have our milk, butter, eggs, and fresh bread delivered right to our house. My mother started this as she had four children at home with no second car, so she felt the basics were important to keep in the house for a constantly hungry growing family like hers. She called on our local home-delivery system vendors and local businesses that catered to help her.

We first started with Sunlite Dairy for our fresh milk and butter, but after a few years, she changed to our local Osborne Dairy, whose farm was located out on a five-mile road on our old state road US 2 before I-75 was built. "We know the family and like supporting people we know," she said about the change. Then she contacted an elderly Dutchman, a true gentleman from Rudyard. His name was Mr. Bestemann. He delivered the fresh eggs, and they were good or better than the ones we would have to buy at our local Red Owl Supermarket. Every two weeks, he delivered the eggs. He would come to our back door and holler out, "Your aaa-eggs!" and he would put them inside in the kitchen. Finally, the staple that was needed was bread—two loaves of it every week. She settled on fresh bread from across the St. Mary's River, baked at the Bluebird Bakery Plant located on Albert Street. This was the bread she ate when she was a child growing up in Soo Ontario. The bakery gave her the name and phone number of our local deliveryman. He was called Dutch, and we were to become his new customer. We knew him a little bit as he lived in the East End. All the boys in the neighborhood liked him. He was always friendly. He had two little girls, and one of them became a great friend with my little sister Kathy; her name was Polly.

He drove a huge van with a large bluebird painted on the side of it. We knew it was coming. Every day, it was jam-packed with fresh, warm bread and rolls and other delights from the bakery. You could smell it coming blocks away. Sometimes, we would follow it to see if he had any doughnuts or sweet bread to give away as samples. His mistake was he did it a few times, and typical of little kids, we overplayed our welcome. We still liked him anyway, even when he barked at us for begging. But he never told on us to our parents.

5. Going to the Wigwam for a Fish Fry

As kids growing up in the East End, we were raised in the traditions of the Catholic Church. My mother's parents and family were deeply devoted French Catholics, and my father's Irish parents were deeply devout Catholics as well. Both sets of grandparents made sure that Dad and Mom and their grandchildren would follow the church's teachings and Catholic traditions. One of our traditions was sacrifice. So on Fridays, meals were to be without meat. There was always fasting too, beginning on a Saturday evening if we wanted to receive the Holy Communion at mass on Sunday. It all seemed complicated to me, but our mother truly believed our little sacrifice was nothing what our Lord did for us. "We should always be mindful of that point," she would say.

The best part of the entire tradition, though, was that we could eat fish. We could, in fact, eat as much as we wanted, according to our tradition. The fish fries throughout the Soo region were quite popular, growing up in the fifties, and they were always on a Friday evening. As I said before, we had a large Catholic community. Some of our neighbors were Protestants and, at times, would tease us. While they were enjoying their steaks and hamburgers, they didn't know how we were enjoying the fact that we had to eat fish.

There were lots of places that had a Friday-evening fish fry. There were at least three that we tried, but we really focused on just two and really enjoyed just one. Our favorite was the Wigwam Restaurant. The other two were the Elks Lodge on Portage Street in town, and the other was Lazy Bob's right by the Whiskey River Bridge out in Brimley. The Wigwam was a bit of a drive to a little rural area called Barbeau. We had to drive south on Riverside Drive down the St. Mary's River. It was always a lovely drive going down the river. Barbeau was originally a small French settlement with its own Catholic Church. It was mostly a farming community at that time, but it had a great restaurant called the Wigwam.

As my dad pulled into the parking lot of the Wigwam, the smells were so inviting of the fish frying we jumped out of the car as quickly as we could to stand in line for our table and seats. We kids were plenty hungry from the drive.

It was fun, though. They served whitefish, walleye, and trout, and their specialty was all-you-could-eat perch. They had some great coleslaw and potato salad too that our mother and father liked. Mom and Dad would just order their dinner. Dad would love his trout, and always, Mother liked whitefish. But my brother John and older sister, Mary, being the ringleaders as they always were, had my little sister, Kathleen, and me order perch like they were doing. They brought us plenty. We stuffed ourselves, and we didn't talk or mention the rest of the evening about how these Catholic traditions of ours were so bad. After all, we were Catholics, and we were different. We often laughed about it. But boy, did we ever enjoy eating that perch.

6. Clyde's Drive-In

It was always special fun when Dad and Mom wanted to drive down Riverside Drive and go to Clyde's Hamburger Stand for dinner. It had a funny name, we thought as kids, but it was literally a hamburger stand, although I guess six people could sit inside and eat if they wanted. As kids, it was all about eating a great hamburger and some fries. Having one of their great chocolate milk shakes with the burger in the car was a special treat. But then came the real fun: sitting down by the St. Mary's River with its large rocks where the ferryboat to Sugar Island used for docking made it just perfect. We enjoyed eating there while watching the ships and feeding the seagulls. There was also a little island attached, and our parents enjoyed going to Rotary Park, as it was called. We could park the car and look at the various boats coming up the river heading through the locks. We called them boats, but they were seven-hundred- foot ships carrying cargo or picking it up from the ore mines and grain ports along Lake Superior. We enjoyed being there a great deal. We enjoyed sitting at the picnic tables, playing our kids games.

What I enjoyed the most, though, was, it was a great time for each parent to tell a few stories of their lives. Dad would tell us stories about the ship he was on during WWII in the South Pacific, the USS General

H.L. Scott, and how it rolled over the large twenty-five- to thirty-foot waves in the Pacific. We, of course, with our questions, wanted him to compare it to sailing on the Great Lakes. All of us, growing up in the Soo, heard many times from older sailors of the storms and waves on Lake Superior. He had a great answer, I always thought: "Once a sailor experiences twenty-five- to thirty-foot waves, it doesn't matter where, it scares you to the bones." We knew the waves were fierce and dangerous on the lake, but it was nice hearing Dad's view. Mom would point out different places across the river in Soo Canada we could see from where we were. She played in those places with her sister when she was a little girl our age, she said. We asked her questions too about whom she played with and what Grandma was like then—just silly-kid questions—but really, you can imagine how important they were at that time to us. It was a great way to know our mom and dad outside the home, and I know we all liked it. Going to Clyde's was more than just fun; I always thought it was special too.

7. Fresh Farm Apple Pie Right from Ma's Orchard

My father's parents, our grandparents, you may recall—we referred to always as Pop and Ma. They were married on August 1, 1915, and had four children in the process, but two of their sons died. One was my namesake, Robert Michael, who lived for six months but died from pneumonia. The other child they named John was stillborn.

My dad used to say, "It was fun growing up on the farm," but still "it was a very difficult life." Pop had worked in the family-owned business, the McCarthy Sawmill, with his brothers Mike and Bill, scratching out a living, while Ma ran the farm, planting and growing crops with help from Dad and his sister Doine. Her real love was her apple orchard— twenty-two different apple trees—that she planted and nursed and groomed herself. She would sell the apples to homes of friends in the village of Pickford and to the local grocer to bring money into the farm. But how that lovely woman could cook a homemade apple pie on that old woodstove "would make you get up in the middle of the night to laugh," my father would say. In other words, it was very good. Really, it was more than that—it was darn good.

In Ma's kitchen, she had a large wooden bowl of several kinds of apples on her wooden kitchen table. But the ones she wanted to bake she separated and placed in a big pan of water while she peeled and sliced and diced the apples for her pie. She had Jonathans, crab, transparent, sour greens, McIntosh, Gala, Golden Delicious, Red Delicious, Granny's, and a special big green apple she called winter apples. These winter apples made the best pies; and those pies, she enjoyed baking for us.

I remember her old woodstove; it was called a Monarch cast iron. It had a big warming oven on top with the firebox on the left side. Right in the middle was the oven itself.

She wouldn't let me slice or dice the winter apples because her paring knife was very sharp and she didn't want me cutting myself. So I enjoyed watching her every move, and of course, I had my thousand questions, something you would expect from a five-year-old boy.

She was so good as I think about her today and so much like Pop. She too loved her grandchildren, and I thought, with her, I was very special. She made me feel that way.

She talked with me through everything she was going to do. The very first thing that needed to be done was build a very hot fire. When she wasn't talking to me, she was singing and humming a song, moving around her kitchen. She had a nice, sweet voice, I thought. There was plenty of cut logs and kindling lying on an old board next to the stove. I remember seeing plenty of bark and leaves lying among the wood. She knew how to build a fire, and within a few minutes, it got so hot in the kitchen we had to open the old swinging door and let some fresh air in.

She had a special way of shuffling her feet back and forth across the kitchen floor. We had to wait thirty to forty-five minutes for the oven to be in the right temperature. She kept a big temperature gauge in the stove hanging down. She knew that woodstove. You really could tell as she tinkered with her fire to keep the temperature the same. She was really an artist, I thought, as I watched her work to put the pie in the oven. The aromas and smells were wonderful, and they worked their way throughout the entire farmhouse. The aroma was so strong even Dad would visit the kitchen and know right off what kind of apple pie his mother was cooking. When the pie was finished, it was a lovely large golden-brown pie. She always let me have the first piece. It had such a beautiful taste. It was something very special—a time I will always remember and a smell I will never forget.

Ma's Song

O, My Love is like a red, red rose,
That's newly sprung in June.
O, My love is like a melodie,
That's sweetly play'd in tune.

As fair thou art my bonnie lass,
So deep in love am I,
And I will love you still, my dear,
Till a' the seas gang dry.

So fare thee well, my only luv,
And fare thee well awhile,
And I will come again my love,
Tho it were ten thousand mile.

(Robert Burns, "A Red, Red Rose")

8. The Longest Clothesline in the East End

I do believe, and I would be willing to bet, that we McCarthys on Cedar Street had the longest clothesline in the East End. It had to be one hundred feet long, if not longer. My brother and I tied a pulley system up from the corner of our backdoor entrance we called the shed. It went diagonally across our backyard to one of our large maple trees. My mother loved hanging clothes out on the line "instead of using electricity," as she would say. But the smell of fresh clothes and sheets and pillowcases is truly worth remembering. It just filled up the house with such wonderful aromas. We all enjoyed it. The funny part was, not one of us barked or complained when our mother asked us to "take in the fresh clothes." It seemed, though, that my brother and I were always the ones to do so while my sisters Mary and Kathleen were supposed to fold and iron them in nice, neat piles as my mother wanted.

That seemed to work most of the time until my lovely sister Mary would not fold my clothes or even iron them; she would just throw them in a pile. I used to complain to her, just to her, and not our mother. Mary would remind me how I was teasing her just the day before. This was her way of getting even with her little brother, and she said I better behave. I thought, though, she just wanted me to obey her. Now remember, she was going to be the nun, and she was just practicing on me, or so I thought. My clothes stayed fresh but wrinkled.

I think that's what started the sibling wars between her and me. They lasted for years. We both always wanted to get the last shot in. The next time I was asked by our mother to bring in the clothes as the rain was coming, I left all of Mary's clothes on the line. But I made certain that everyone else had theirs freshly dried. When it was my sister's turn to iron and fold our clothes, Mary saw that none of the clothes were hers. I told her, hers were on the line and they were all wet from the rain. Well, the whole house exploded. We all knew she was not a happy little girl. She was always bigger than me, and this sister-brother squabble went on for years between us. After the scolding from Mom, life went on. I ended it all by paying Mary a nickel each time she ironed my clothes. She wouldn't do it unless I paid her. My sister and I broke windows and mirrors and had several food fights, and there's no question that we drove both our parents crazy. But she has always been my partner at so many things, and we are close as mud today.

9. Ice Fishing

Today on eBay or Amazon, you can be outfitted with the greatest sports equipment ever, especially if you like to go ice fishing. There are huts today that new advancements in technology will all but guarantee and assure the owner and his/her friends a success at fishing in two to three feet of frozen water. Compared to how we did it in the 1950s, we were really in the ice age.

An ice shanty, as we knew it—or, as some call it in the Soo, an ice shack—was really a portable shed placed on a frozen lake to provide shelter during ice fishing. They could be as small and cheap as a plastic tarp draped over a frame of two-by-fours or as expensive as a small cabin with heat, bunks, electricity, and cooking facilities. When we went ice fishing with our friend Bob Ermatinger, we were in an eight-foot square hut built of wood, and we thought we were in heaven. We had several jiggers, two spears, a big auger we had to use manually, some bait, and some food we could heat up in the shanty.

You have to understand: we lived in the Sault, and like so many northern communities, ice fishing was not just a sport; it was a winter culture. It was a traditional winter pastime in our Great Lakes region, and we had homemade wooden shacks like ours dotting the frozen waters in Cedarville.

Every year, we helped Bob move his nice ice shanty to Les Cheneaux Islands in Cedarville. We placed it on sleds and hauled it by ropes to a location about a half mile off the shore. Every year, Bob felt he found the perfect location to jig for perch or spear a bigger fish like pike and even whitefish.

In northern climates, ice shanties are the center of a large folklore. Bob would always say as we were setting our shanty up that "every lake has at least one ice shanty on the bottom." The Les Cheneaux had several of them, he would say.

The fun always started at 4:00 a.m. as we drove out to Cedarville. We took that cold half-mile walk across the ice to the shanty. We brought a lantern crossing the dark ice, but several times, the moon was bright enough that we didn't need the lantern. But it was still cold. It was very cold. When we arrived, Bob would immediately start our Coleman stove to heat up the shack. We then began to auger a two-foot-by- four-foot section of our ice that we previously cut out as we laid up the shanty. Then we were ready. Jigging for perch was easy and fun. You could see them in schools, and you were right there to catch them. We caught them in bunches, but throwing those spears was very unique and very different for me. We could see the larger fish. They were staying down by the bottom, which made it nearly impossible to stick one. We tried anyway, and at least Bob tailed one that had to be twelve feet deep. Then all of a sudden, a twenty-eight-inch whitefish came cruising by our open slab of ice, and boom, we got it. All you could say is, wow, was that ever exciting.

10. Kaine's Rink

Kids today playing hockey don't know how good they have it. What are there, four to five practice rinks in the Soo today? In the fifties, we had two; that's it. We had the Pullar and Kaine's Rink. Sure, we had lots of outdoor and backyard rinks, and yes, back then, we didn't have the extended shipping season, so hundreds of kids skated in the lower St. Mary's River, and that was a real hoot. We skated for miles, but there was nothing like the ice at Kaine's Rink. The building known as Kaine's Rink was originally a streetcar barn, then with the demise of the streetcars, it was acquired by Mr. John Kaine, who converted it into a boiler and machine shop. After a few years in this capacity, Mr. Kaine, an ardent hockey fan, converted it again—this time, into the Soo's only indoor ice rink. For a while during the 1930s, it was the scene of many thrilling hockey matches but was forced out of business with the completion of the Pullar Community Building in 1939.

During this time, it was becoming increasingly apparent to the City Recreation Department that the city maintaining outside rinks was not providing enough ice time to develop the younger skaters into the ice-skaters and hockey players capable of successfully competing in the Pullar Community Building and other ice arenas through the country and over into Ontario in Canada.

In November 1955, members of the (City) Recreation Commission met with a member of the Kaines family. It was agreed upon that the Recreation Department could have Kaine's Rink on a rental basis for use of hockey and skating and for any other use as was seen fit. With the death of John Kaine, the rental was changed to a purchase basis and adopted by the City Commission.

On January 11, 1963, Anna C. Kaine, widow of John Kaine, deeded the property and building to the city of Sault Sainte Marie for a consideration of one dollar.

I would bet that almost every hockey player in town started or played there. Everyone who wanted to play hockey during the fifties started there. It was an outdoor rink in truth; although it had walls and a roof, it was naturally cold and smelled how a real rink should because it was so cold.

In the summers, the city would open Kaine's to roller-skating and, at times, parties. But most of the time, the Pullar was the main attraction for all those summer activities. It was always the place in town for our youth to go.

But by winter, we all got ready for where all the little guys played— Kaine's Rink. It was totally different from skating on the ice at the Pullar. This was like skating on a much-bigger outdoor rink and was much different from skating on our river.

Over the years, thousands of kids skated there and got started there. They began their dream of playing hockey right there. Some of our youth from the Soo climbed pretty high, playing hockey. They all got their start on Kaine's Rink.

11. Playing in Our Hay Barn

Our big home on 706 Cedar Street was built in the 1880s, and of course, we had a very large garage. In fact, it was a very large horse barn that was converted to an auto barn when cars became part of the Sault society. In the second story, there was a large hayloft where the hay was stored through a large swinging door. It had two large feeder shoots (holes in the floor) to feed the horses from above. Even when we moved there in the fifties, it smelled like an old hay barn. There were still old pieces of dried hay we had to sweep up if we wanted to play there, and we did.

As kids, we played for hours up there in that hayloft. We would climb the stepladder, which was built into the wall of the barn, right next to where the horses were tied. There was an old steel rail bolted into beams of the barn, and we kept the harnesses and the old ropes that tied down the horses when they were feeding. It was a fun place to dream of older times, of how life used to be. To us, it was just a safe and fun place to play. The nasty part was how dirty we would all get because it was truly an old horse barn.

Throughout the various seasons, we enjoyed jumping out of the hayloft door. It was just fifteen feet up, so no one would get hurt. In the autumn, we would stack up piles of our leaves, and we had plenty of those. We would pile the leaves in bundles up to eight feet high and just lunge out into the leaves from the barn, jumping feetfirst. All of us would do it. My sisters, I thought, were brave and bold, and they had fun doing what we boys did. We were proud of our sisters because they were the first girls to do so in our neighborhood.

In the winter, we did the same thing. We piled up the snow as high as we could shovel it, but in the snow, we could be more reckless by jumping out of the loft butt first. It was fun, and everyone in the neighborhood used that for our winter activity when we weren't playing hockey or shinny or skating or sledding. It was playing in McCarthy's barn. These were certainly simpler times when we compare it to today, but my goodness, we had fun. When we finished, we all smelled like old hay.

> This house is old, it carries on
> Like lyrics to an old time song,
> Always changed but never gone,
> This house can stand the seasons.
>
> Our live's pass on from door to door
> Like dust across a wooden floor,
> Feather rain or thunder roar,
> We need not know the difference.
>
> (David Mallett, "I Knew This Place")

12. Warner's Bakery—the Best Cinnamon Rolls Ever

There are many kinds of bakeries that specialize in many different kinds of baked goods and other things—things such as fresh dinner rolls and various kinds of sweet bread, sourdough bread, cinnamon rolls, and of course, all kinds of doughnuts. There were always other baked goods such as pies and cakes. Of course, you could get a Coca-Cola or a hot chocolate. I thought the best bakeries had a good hot chocolate. We had three bakeries in the Soo then, but I always thought the best of the best was Warner's Bakery on E. Portage Street. If you can remember where Godin's Sports Store and Dorgan's Takeout were and if you can remember where the old Majestic Hotel was—right near the old Sault Savings Bank—that's where you would find the best bakery in the Soo. My dad loved going there as it was very close to the bank he worked in at that time, and business leaders would gather there for morning coffee. So Dad knew the owners and the family pretty well.

He would bring us there on Saturday mornings, and the highlight and specialties were their cinnamon rolls and breads. But as a little boy, I thought they had the best doughnuts in the world. Everyone always commented on their great cinnamon rolls, but I thought their homemade doughnuts were the very best. They were that good. My brother enjoyed the cinnamon rolls and ate as many as he possibly could, while I liked their doughnuts. My taste buds today still bring me back to the age of seven when I had my first doughnut there with a small hot chocolate. Every time today I walk into a doughnut shop or a bakery, I remember those strong smells and lovely aroma coming from those delicious breads and cakes and how it made me feel. The shops today are good, but they don't carry a candle to Warner's Bakery or the fond memories I have of eating those delicious doughnuts.

It was also a place where all the old men gathered before a big hockey game at the Pullar. It served a multipurpose really for the hometowners. I know when our visitors came over on the ferryboats from Canada, people always stopped there. The Canadians sure enjoyed eating there. One day, my brother and I had a contest; my brother and I always had food contests. This one was how many cinnamon rolls he could eat versus how many doughnuts I could eat. He won, but when we both got home, we both got sick. The memory of Warner's Bakery is as fresh today as ever. I remember those delicious, old-fashioned doughnuts, and I can smell the aroma from their kitchen, and my mouth starts watering. That's a memory to keep. And their cinnamon rolls were pretty good too.

13. McCarthy Easter Egg–Eating Contest

Since we were little kids, we all heard of the stories from Pop and then our father of the famous Easter egg–eating contest among the McCarthys. This was an egg-eating contest between Pop and all his brothers and sisters. Pop had eight siblings before they came to the United States.

They lived on a farm in Alliston, Ontario, just outside of Toronto, and "we had plenty of chickens" as Pop would say. On Easter Sunday morning, the family of three brothers and five sisters—all of them—had a family contest. The food contest was who could eat the most eggs: poached, fried, or scrambled. The winner who ate the most eggs was crowned Easter champion. We liked the story because it involved both the brothers and sisters and everyone participated. The numbers were huge; we thought as Uncle Mike, Pop's younger brother, ate thirty-five eggs, followed by Uncle Bill, the baby of their family, at thirty-one. Pop had twenty-seven. The sisters all dropped out early, but his oldest sister, Liz, ate nine eggs.

To us as kids, it sounded like fun, so we agreed. We all had to try it. We would crown our own Easter champion from our McCarthy family. There was John and myself and my sisters Mary and Kathleen. Both Dad and Mom cooked, and we all started with three scrambled eggs each; everyone passed the first test. We as kids were giggling and laughing, and we all joined in on the fun. The second round was the poached eggs on toast, and then the girls dropped out. Kathleen was the first, but she was the youngest; and after eating just two poached eggs, she had to quit. Mary finished her poached eggs, and that was all she could do as she couldn't go any further. John and I were proud as punch that we were still in the competition. Now, it was time for fried eggs. Dad would make them over easy or sunny-side up. John liked his over easy, and I wanted mine sunny-side up. We were going strong as we both got to twelve eggs. But we both knew we were never going to tie Pop's brothers and sisters. Everyone was roaring and laughing, and it was great fun being there in our kitchen. Our parents, especially our mother, were pleading with us not to get sick. Dad just kept on encouraging us as he liked the competition and enjoyed the cooking. Pop was just shaking his head and smiling; you could see he was enjoying it all.

John finished the contest as the declared Easter champion with a total of eighteen eggs while I ate fifteen. The nicest part was, no one got sick, although we couldn't eat until the next day. The funniest part, though, was how much we enjoyed talking about it and reliving it. Having Pop and Dad and even our mother carry on the story about the new version of the McCarthy family Easter egg–eating contest was something we really enjoyed. All that was fine, but we never did it again. At the end of it all, Pop would be humming a tune that he always enjoyed singing when the laughter and chitchat of the family was at its peak. And we would all join in. It was quite an event for sure.

Pop's Song at the McCarthys' Party

A noble man you see, if you'll only look at me,

The other day I met McCarthy walking down the way. He did say to me, "won't you come to my party,

The folks to be sure, will be crowded to the door." We'll all be gay and hearty, at McCarthy's party, We'll all let down our hair.

Murphy's, Burke's and Leahy's, will be there, Where? (J. E. Murphy, "Down at McCarthy's Party" [1882])

14. The Carbide Dust on a Windy Day

I remember driving down East Portage Avenue with my mother after grade school early in the spring of the year, and as we crossed the Portage Street Bridge, you could easily see that the rows of houses were all gray, and some were really darkened. Whether it was Portage, Barbeau, Sova, Maple, Cedar, or Spruce Streets, the carbide dust hit us all, and it lay over the entire East End of our town. I mean, all our homes were covered. You could see that even the roofs and windows of the homes were gray colored as well. This was a regular occurrence when the northern wind was blowing across the river from our Canadian cousins. Our carbide plant was churning out carbide dust that would certainly cause you to blink and rub your eyes. It was that plentiful. It would burn the eyes a little bit too.

The wintertime was just as bad. Don't you remember seeing the black- covered snowbanks when you were driving through the East End? Some people thought innocently that was just the salt and sand poured on the road splashing up and discoloring our snowbanks. The locals, however, knew better. Our carbide dust landed and darkened our snow, and we couldn't wait for a fresh new snowfall to brighten them up again.

The worst part was getting that darn dust on your clothes and in your mouth. It smelled horrible and tasted worse. It wasn't as bad as the lime piles, but everyone in the East End had to regularly wash their homes with their water hose just to get the dust off their house.

Two things you needed to do right away: First, make sure all your windows were closed as the dust would find its way into your house. Second, if you had any wet clothes on the line, you better get them off quickly, as your mom would be washing them again.

The breeze would eventually let up by early evening and give everyone a chance to clean things up a bit. On the weekends, it seemed everyone in the East End was washing their cars and spraying their homes and windows with hose water.

The St. Mary's River gave us lots of smells: fish, our paper mill, our tannery, and our own carbide. But we always seemed to smile through it all and knew that tomorrow, the river would bring us a different wind.

15. The Great Moose Lodge Fire of 1961

On January 27, 1961, early in the morning, what started out to be a normal call to our fire department as a small flame spread like wildfire. One of our city's largest buildings was the Moose Lodge. It had several apartments upstairs in addition to the lodge itself. It was known locally as the Brown Block on South Ashmun Street. The fire lasted twenty- four hours, and it consumed the businesses next to it, both Sherwin- Williams Paints and Hallesy's Bar. All fourteen of the apartments and the lodge were left in ashes after the fire ended. Everything was burned to the ground.

The volume of black smoke roiled and boiled for hours. It was reported afterward that it was one of the greatest fires in the history of the Soo in the last one hundred years. I was in seventh grade by then, and I was there. I watched it for hours with my dad and older brother, John. It was a cold winter day. Supposedly, the fire started in one of the apartments. The occupant was gone, but something electrical was left on, and the rest they say is history. Fortunately, no one was injured as it happened during the morning hours. Everyone was asked to evacuate immediately. The flames from that four-story building shot up to the sky, and the clouds of smoke gushing from the building were heavy— extremely heavy. The firemen with their fire trucks and their extension ladders were busy as can be. Their partners on the ground were moving fire hoses left and right and keeping people back safely from the flames. We stood back some distance, across the street, and although it was cold out, you could feel the heat from the burning building. You could really smell different things burning inside the lodge and stores. To us as observers, it was so apparent, especially when the fire started inside the Sherwin-Williams Paint Store. The smell of burning paint with all those added chemicals was causing the firemen to be very cautious as an explosion could very easily occur.

Our uncle Elgar, on my mother's side, worked there when he wasn't working on the tugboats. We all thought and hoped he was home. My father called him at home to be sure and spoke with him. He was coming back down to the fire as he was there earlier trying to get things out of the lodge when the fire department told everyone they needed to evacuate because the fire was spreading fast. He needed to get home as he too had a young family. My cousins were younger than myself. He felt they all would be scared. We were still there when my uncle Elgar came up beside us. He mentioned to Dad how the firemen were very worried about an explosion and having the fire run on them and jump the street where we were standing. They said the fire could very easily start something at our Soo Creamery, which had a large dairy facility just a block up from the Brown Block, also on Ashmun Street. A crew was put on alert out in front of the creamery, ready for any spark or flame. We called it the Brown Block because the building, when it was built, was the Brown Building, a gorgeous new building to the growing landscape of the Soo.

There are two things that have shaped my memory about this fire. First is the flames. They were so large, and they soared so high. They kept climbing higher and higher. Second is the deep-black smoke. I thought it just wasn't smoke; it couldn't be with all those smells. They were all so very strong.

It took a full twenty-four hours to burn itself out, and it was a history to be noted. But no one we knew wanted to remember that kind of history. It was a start of bad news for our little town, which was coming from our carbide and tannery plants and our own Camp Lucas, which would change my town forever.

16. Mary Maude Payment—our Feisty, Loving Grandmother

by Mary McCarthy and Kathleen McCarthy Adams

Our grandmother Mary Maude Payment Trempe was truly a force of nature. She was tiny—four feet ten inches—but a powerful woman. We called her Gramma. As a young teenager and even into her sixties, she wore her hair in braids around her head that framed two sharp black eyes. The Ursuline Sisters at St. Ignace, Michigan, raised her from the time she was two years old after her mother, an Algonquin Indian woman named Rose from the Garden River reservation in Ontario, died of pneumonia. Her father, Felix, wanted his daughter to be raised in the French Catholic tradition. Her family, the Payments, was a very large family that came to the Sault in the early 1800s from Quebec. They were boatbuilders and carpenters from the west coast of France. Most or all members of the family lived in the small hamlet of Payment on Sugar Island, Michigan. Young Mary stayed with the nuns, going to school there until she was fourteen. During the summers, she would come home to the Sault, making the fifty-mile trip by horse and buggy. She lived with her father and brother, Clementine, in the house her father had built at 810 Cedar Street in the Sault. She later returned to that same house when her own family was raised.

Through the early fifties, when our family was young, we lived in the house at 810 in the downstairs apartment while Gramma and Grandpa lived upstairs with our bachelor uncle, Uncle Henny. We grew up seeing Gramma every day and had plenty of time for chatting, watching her cook and clean, and taking baths in their big claw-foot bathtub.

Gramma was always ready for a laugh or a funny story. Even as kids, we thought she was an odd partner for our grandpa Trempe—a staid, quiet Frenchman with a drop of dry-humored English ancestry. Married over fifty years, living in both Sault Ontario and Sault Michigan, they raised nine children. Our mother, Frances, was their seventh child. They survived the death of two young girls, the Great Depression, two world wars, and Grandpa's nervous breakdown. When Grandpa became ill, the doctor insisted he needed to "rest his nerves," so he went to New York to stay with his wealthy sister, Aunt Belle. He left Gramma with "seven mouths to feed," as she would say. The doctor who treated Grandpa said she could work for him as he traveled to patients' homes. Gramma soon became known as a healer herself. Her days were spent traveling with the doctor as his nurse and then coming home to mind her own family and household duties. As little girls, we were always so proud of our gramma's strength and tenacity and wanted to be like her.

Gramma, due to the nuns who raised her, was deeply religious and devoted to the Lord Jesus and his Blessed Mother, for whom she was named. She really did trust in God and daily recited the rosary. Gramma would tell us that often when money was low and a bill needed paying, she prayed her rosary, and sure enough, like a small miracle, the next day, an insurance claim check or some other windfall would come in the mail.

Gramma had the reputation as a "kindhearted" lady. In front of her home during the Depression was painted a hobo cat symbol, which was a sign to tramps—those who were unemployed and homeless—that at this house, "riders of the rail" would be given food or work. The symbol was their way of passing information through an underground network to others coming after them. Gramma always found some chores the men could do and in payment be given food before sending them on their way.

Kathy's Remembrance

One of the things I learned as a young girl about my grandmother was, despite being small, she was feisty. That and her religious devotion were traits that served her well. Gramma was a real survivor. She used to tell me the story of getting married to my grandfather at sixteen. "He fell in love with me right away," she would say. "I know it was my long wavy black hair and my two deep-black eyes. That was what caught his eye," she would tell me. "Your mother, Frances, has those same eyes like mine, and I will bet that did it for your dad too." Shortly after their wedding, one of the town busybodies asked Gramma if she had to get married, and she promptly and very naively faced the woman and replied, "Yes." Hearing this shocked my Catholic schoolgirl sensibilities, and she quickly explained herself to me. She had to get married, she said, since her father gave Grandpa his blessing and permission. "So of course, I had to marry Henry." She couldn't let her father down. She chuckled, remembering how that rude woman kept checking for a sign of pregnancy each time she saw her. "Hah," she told me, "it was two years before I had my first baby."

One day, when I was around eleven, as I was playing outside the big house at 706 Cedar where we now are living, an ambulance sped down our street with its sirens blaring. This was very odd for our quiet street. A neighborhood friend ran up to me saying that the ambulance was at my gramma's house. I yelled for my mother, and within seconds, she was in the car racing down the driveway. I grabbed my bike and followed her as fast as I could. We just lived a block away, and I remember thinking that maybe it was a neighbor's child that was hurt and had been brought to Gramma's for help. When I got to the house, my eyes went directly to Gramma, who was struggling and twisting on the sofa. Her face was an odd shade of gray, and it showed extreme pain. My mother was there beside her praying while the paramedics worked on Gramma. They whisked her off in the ambulance within minutes. Mother told me to get home as she sped off for the hospital.

Gramma survived the heart attack and recovered overtime. She continued to be our family matriarch for another decade, and she took time with each of us—all twenty of her grandchildren. She showed us love and passed her words of wisdom to us. "God love her (or him)" was her favorite saying. If any critical words were said about anyone, she would always end it with these words as if to neutralize the sting of any harshness. We all still say this and laugh. And we laugh when we remember her insisting on holding our hands while walking to church or through the Red Owl. We laugh remembering how she would walk to church down the middle of Cedar Street for the 7:00 a.m. mass right by our house with her chin up, wanting to be called in for a ride to church—never asking, of course. We still recall the advice she gave us as young girls to always carry a three-inch hatpin in our hands, ready to fend off any attacker, as she did.

Mary's Remembrance

Our grandparents had a hospital bed in their apartment upstairs, and that's where Gramma placed her patient—whoever in the family was sick at that time. I remember getting my tonsils out when I was six and how important I felt lying in that fancy bed, having Gramma nurse me, only me. No one dared question her authority on the issue of our health. I will always remember the gargling with salt water, the Vicks VapoRub, the kissing on the forehead to feel for fever, the cupping of my neck for swollen glands, and even the dreaded enema. Not only myself but also all my brothers and sister knew we were safe in Gramma's healing hands. And we always were.

Gramma never smoked until she turned sixty-two years old. At that time, ferryboats used to transport people across the river to and from the twin Saults. Gramma used to go over and back often as her children lived on both sides of the river. One evening, when returning, as it approached the dock, the ferryboat hit the pier head-on, and Gramma was tossed several feet, landing directly on her shoulder and arm. The accident caused a break in her upper arm and gave her severe pain. In those days, she was given morphine for the pain and found she soon became addicted. The doctor, in an effort to get her off the drug, suggested she start smoking instead. And did she smoke! Her house, we noted, not only smelled of cooked cabbage and dampness, but it now was added with the distinct choking aroma of Larks, Gramma's favorite brand. She'd say that the charcoal filtered out the bad stuff. Every time I came home from college, I'd stop at Gramma's with packs of Larks for her and me to smoke together as we gossiped about family and movie stars. We coughed and laughed through many a visit. (I was new to smoking then myself.)

My last memory of Gramma exemplifies her life to me. She was in the hospital dying of liver cancer, ironically, as she never drank any alcohol. I came to see her from out of town, and I was eight months pregnant with my son Brian at that time. I saw her shriveled little body on the hospital bed and broke down sobbing as I went to her. She took my hand and comforted me, saying, "Mary, stop now. You have to think of your baby, dear."

And she like a ghost beside me, goes down with ease of a dolphin. And emerges unlearned, unshamed, unharmed.

For she is a perfect creature, natural in every feature, And I am the geek with the alchemists stone.

(Jimmy McCarthy, "One Bright Blue Rose")

Thinking about her now, we can see that in every moment of her life, she considered the needs of others over her own. She would be the first to say she was not a saint, but her grandchildren would say differently. We are deeply grateful to have known this force of nature so intimately over the years. Her presence is still felt in each of our hearts, lightening them with laughter and filling them with the tenderness of love. What greater gift can anyone give?

Ave Maria

Ave Maria, gracia plena,
Dominus tecum, benedicta tu in mulieibus,
Et benedictus fructus ventris tui Jesus,
Sancta Maria, mater Dei,
Ora pro nobis peccatoribus,
Nunc, et in hora u nostrae.

Amen

(Franz Schubert, Latin edition [1825])

Final Chapter of Smells

17. Saying Goodbye to Pop

Our grandfather, whom we called Pop, died March 15, 1959. My dad was extremely close to him. He always called him Pop; he called him sometimes Dad and oftentimes the old man. When Pop passed, it was more than a sad, sad day. It was my very first experience of feeling a deep emotional loss. It was the worst St. Patrick's Day celebration I have ever experienced just two days later. But most importantly, I lost my dear friend. It is true that grandparents help raise their grandchildren. We saw that on both sides of our family with Grandma Trempe, our mother's mother, whom we dearly loved, and definitely with Pop. I felt he helped raise me.

> The tears have all been shed now,
> We've said our last goodbye.
> His soul's been blessed, and his laid to rest,
> But it's now I feel alone.
> He was more than just my father,
> My teacher, my best friend.
> And the tunes we shared will still be heard,
> When I sing them on my own.

(Phil Coulter, "The Old Man")

He was born in Canada in Alliston, Ontario, in 1875. His father, also named John, was born on one of the Irish coffin ships bringing famine immigrants over to the United States to begin a new life. They were called coffin ships because as much as 40 percent of those traveling would die from sickness and starvation. His birth was registered in Albany, New York. His parents immediately headed north to Canada as land was coming available to homestead and the lumber boom was in its early years. There, John met an Irishwoman. They were married, and off they went to Alliston, Ontario, to follow the lumber boom happening in Ontario. Pop was their firstborn and the eldest son of nine children.

He had a colorful life, I thought. He was a lumberjack, and throughout his business and work life, he followed the white pine industry in Northern and Upper Michigan and Canada. His father too was an expert sawyer and lumberman. Grandpa McCarthy (whom we called Pop's dad) and his three sons, Pop, Mike, and Bill, operated a portable sawmill and kept a small group of Irish immigrants and Native Americans working for them outside the Rockview cut near the village of Pickford. "Life was pretty good," Pop said to my father, until the accident that killed his father at the mill. The man he called in the Irish, Da. Grandpa McCarthy was the head sawyer and a good one, Pop said. One day, a slab of a huge pine log discharged while going through its first cut and fired backward at full force, speed killing Pop's father. Pop would try to remember the events of that day, but the years had cemented what happened next. Pop left and just walked away for five years. "The hurt was so deep," my father said. "He couldn't face it and didn't want to face it." He too was very close to his father and was still a single man in his early thirties when his father was buried.

The McCarthy Sawing Mill

There's wealth in raising cattle,
And there's money made in hay.
The butcher's and the grocer's,
Grow richer everyday.

But there isn't a vocation,
Worked with whatever skill,
Will give its owners pockets,
Like a portable saw mill.

Between Donaldson and Pickford,
And just about half way,

McCarthy's mill's located,
For a temporary stay.

There from morning till the evening,
You'll find a busy throng,
While the circular and the engine,
Sing a wealth producing song.

At seven every morning,
At the welcome hour of noon,
And at six o'clock each evening,
She whistles up a tune.

Like the howling of some wild beast,
In the distant jungle land,
But it has the sound of music,
To her busy hustling band.

Old John stands with the lever,
In his ever ready hand,
While the mill and men together,
Obey his last command.

John Jr. rides the carriage,
Sets the timber for the saw,
While Mike attends the engine,
And the boiler's fiery saw.

John Hanna has the cross cut,
Under his special charge,
And cuts up into stove wood,
All slabs however large.

And John has got the movements,
Intelligence and skill,

To cut more slabs than any man,
That works around the mill.

Hank Johnson's bass tail sawyer,
A lad both strong and quick,
Who very keenly watches,
The slabs are not too thick.

While William draws the timber,
With his doughty well trained team,
And rolls it on the skid way,
There ends my rhyming theme

(H. Duggan, circa 1904)

But those five years were an interesting part of his life. He went from lumber camp to lumber camp working twelve to fourteen hours a day, trying to keep some money in his pockets and just trying to forget his father dying in his arms. The cutting of the native white pine at that time was being done in the Seney/ Shingleton area of the Upper Peninsula of Michigan. Outside of the state of Washington, there were more white pines here than in any place in the country or in Canada. It was said that there was one hundred years of cutting before it would all be gone. These two small lumber towns were halfway between the Soo and Marquette. It was here he spent over three years of his life. Several large lumber camps existed there with the largest camp employing about five hundred men. The camps had their own living quarters and a large dining hall with a small company store. Most of the time, the camps were located near a running river so they could have freshwater. The company always brought in a staff to cook and feed the loggers. Many families living in the UP made a livelihood like this for many years. Most of Pop's humorous stories came from here. He would tell us and show us how the loggers ate their corn on the cob, how they cut their steak with a fork and a spoon, how the men ate their peas and buttered their bread. It was so much fun trying to mimic what Pop did in the logging camps. Mother sometimes would just laugh at us and say, "Now, don't do that out in the public." Our mother loved Pop and truly cared for him as he aged.

And I never will forget him,
For he made me what I am.
Though he may be gone,
Memories linger on,
And I miss him, the old man.

(Phil Coulter, "The Old Man")

As a young boy, Pop had completed just two years of school; "I went to the second book," he would say. So after his father's death, when Pop took off, no one back home—his mother or his siblings in the Tone area where they lived and homesteaded—knew if he was alive or dead. Pop couldn't read or write. So they just waited for him to come back home.

This was the man I tried to recall and keep fresh in my memory when he passed. On the following day of his death, I climbed the biggest tree in our yard and shimmied my way right to the very top of the tree and swung in the spring breeze for hours. I cried nonstop, it seemed. I wanted so much to speak with him again, and for those six hours in that tree, I tried to remember all the stories he told to me and my sisters and brother.

But on the evening he died, my youngest sister, Kathy, and I were playing upstairs near his bedroom. The last several months of his life, he was becoming more bedridden and very weak. The doctor told us he had very little time left and his heart was fading. Mom and Dad and Doine and Dongol wanted him to die at home in his own bed and not in a hospital. My mother, God bless her, said she would nurse him and did. During the day and evening of March 15, the whole family was together doing our vigil at the house on Cedar Street, praying while the local parish priest stopped by to give Pop the last rites. My father's sister was Geraldine; her husband was Donald McDonald. We fondly called them Doine and Dongol and loved them dearly. These folks were the McDonalds, our family. Their kids were Joannie, Danny, and Ruthie; they were our closest cousins.

But it was early in that evening when Kathy and I found him breathing very hard with a long pause between breaths. We ran down the stairs to tell Mom and Dad and Doine and Dongol. They all came upstairs to see immediately. Within fifty minutes, Pop took his last breath, with Kathy and me right there next to him. She was just six years old at that time, but she was holding his hand, while I had my ear listening to his heart, laying my head softly on his chest. Then it was over. It was truly my first experience facing the final chapter of the circle of life, but I thought the smell and odor of death all around us was cold and very lonely and certainly only a time to be sad and solemn. My time too of being a little boy was over; in two years, I would be a teenager. After that, the sounds and smells of my youth started changing. And my world started to get much bigger.

He Walked on Water

He wore colored flannel shirts buttoned at the neck,
and he'd sit in the shade and watch the chickens peck. And
his teeth were gone, but what the heck,
I thought that he walked on water.

He said he was a lumberjack when he was young.
He could handle an ax and he was good with a shotgun. And
my daddy was his oldest son,--
and I thought that he walked on water.

(Randy Travis)

Acknowledgment

As I prepared writing for my second memoir, *The Sounds and Smells of My Childhood—Part II*, four major events took place in my life. Four very important men who greatly influenced the direction of my life were stricken with severe illness or death.

The first man was Dan Dorrity. Dan was a dear personal friend of mine and, just recently, passed away in the Sault. He came to Sault Sainte Marie as a bricklayer from the county Tyrone in Northern Ireland in the fifties. He worked his way through college, and he picked up his PhD in history to teach at our local university. He ran for public office in the seventies and was elected as a Democrat. This was highly unusual at that time in the Soo as Democrats weren't getting elected. He was elected chairman of the county commissioners and took his leadership role personally. Our local economy was hovering at 25 percent unemployment at that time, and we needed action. We also needed courage, and Dan was there. After the closing of the Kincheloe Air Base, Dan led the collaborative effort with the Base Conversion Authority and the Economic Development Corporation that brought about the economic transformation of the Sault and Chippewa County. His efforts have benefited people to this day. He was responsible for my hiring at the EDC, the corporation responsible for recruiting and developing new jobs. Over 1,400 new jobs were developed in the county. Dan will be forever missed.

The second man is Thomas Suddes. Tom was stricken with a severe illness this year. He is very well-known as the two-time boxing champion at Notre Dame University and, later, the boxing coach for several years at the same school. But he is better known as one of Notre Dame University's top development directors that successfully completed their $180 million capital campaign in the early 1980s. Tom and his colleagues at Notre Dame undertook a direct solicitation effort, the first of its kind in the country. It was a major success. Up until then, capital campaigns were utilizing alumni as their main source of solicitation. Every major university in the country did their fund-raising in this manner. Notre Dame changed the formula, and the strategic mind behind that was Tom Suddes. He was the first fund-raiser in the country to change that paradigm, and he had transformed fund-raising ever since. After I left my executive role at the Columbus Chamber of Commerce in the late 1980s, Tom brought me in as one of his five partners under the flag of the Suddes Group. We changed fund-raising for nonprofits in the United States, especially for chambers of commerce and other economic development corporations. Those chambers seeking new capital investment and jobs for their communities knew the Suddes Group could deliver. We raised millions for them. I went on my own eight years later and created both my companies that exist today. Tom is a very special person in my life. He remains a true, loyal friend. He is a fighter, and I pray he wins his latest fight with ALS.

Note: As my book was being sent to the publisher, I received word that Tom lost his battle with ALS. He died September 26, 2016. RIP, my dear friend.

The third was my oldest and dearest friend, Timothy O'Kinney. I have known Tim since I was a young fart of six years old. He was just a year older than me, and we lived as next-door neighbors all throughout grade school and high school. Even as a young boy, he loved adventure, and I enjoyed being with him on many of those exploits. It was fun just hanging out with him. He was a big kid—a very big kid—but he was a funny and a happy kid and always great at any sport he ever tried, it seemed. He was always smiling. My mother so enjoyed him, and she loved his smile and happy spirit.

As he aged, Tim was still looking forward to the next adventure, and people of all kinds and all ages loved to be around him. He is, and was, a special person to me. He was always very protective of his friends, and as a young boy, I felt very safe with him.

He took off for Colorado when he just turned twenty-two and took work in a camera shop in Denver, saving as much money as he could so he could buy a piece of land and build his dream home up in the Rocky Mountains outside Winter Park at an elevation of nine thousand feet. He learned how to be a builder and became one of the most successful builders and developers in the Frazier Valley.

We have stayed close over all these years, and in fact, I moved to Winter Park, and we became neighbors again. In fact, I moved into one of those beautiful homes he built. It was like second nature being together as neighbors again, and it was enjoyable and peaceful.

He is, by far, the most amazing man I have ever met. Tim has always faced health challenges while living his life to the fullest. Accidents of every kind have played havoc on his body, though. Broken ribs, punctured lungs, two new knees, one new hip, and overcoming Hodgkin's lymphoma have been just some. And would you believe that even after his first heart attack two years ago, he snowboarded sixty times last year? But time unfortunately has caught up with him.

Today, Tim is in the biggest fight of his life. He had a recent second heart attack, and with just 10 percent of his heart functioning, he lies in the cardiac unit at the CU Hospital Anschutz Medical Center in Denver, awaiting the final decision for a heart transplant or possibly a mechanical heart.

Tim has been more than a friend. His kind doesn't come around too often in this circle of life, but life is what he brings to those he meets and embraces. My prayers and thoughts are with him, that he pulls through one more time and continues to bless us with his joy for life and enthusiasm for another adventure. He has dreamed his dreams, but Tim Kinney continues to still live them. Long may he continue.

The fourth was my big brother, John, who died suddenly on October 7, 2016. Yes, he was my hero, but he was also my big brother and most trusted friend growing up. He was my knight in shining armor and my brightest shining star. John was the one you could always count on for answers, be they simple or hard, one you could always depend on without an argument or bad word. We shared many of our dreams and plans and some secrets too, but John always told me "like it is" and never wanted to see me lose. He always believed in me.

He had some tough times, especially the last four years, with his health, suffering from severe neuropathy, sugar diabetes, and spinal dystrophy. But he always found a way to fight through them. His closest friend and the love of his life, who was with him until the end, was his dear wife, Jeanette. "His wonderful big heart just couldn't go any further," she told me, and "he went so very fast." He will always hold a very special place in all our hearts that no one else will ever fill. There has always been just the five of us (the brothers and sisters), and now one-fifth of me just disappeared, and I feel my tears will never go away.

He was the strongest man I ever knew—a big man, in his prime, a huge man—but a gentle giant with a child's heart. I never got the chance to say a proper goodbye. My dad used to say, "No one will ever understand you, your craziness, how you think and feel like your older brother, John, does." I certainly can attest to that; that's the way it was for me.

Like the poet once said, "While people come and go in your life, your brother will always be in your heart for a lifetime." No more will we see his warm smile or hear his salute to his brothers and sisters, like "Hi, Marildee" or "How's R. Michael?" and "Hi, Kath, how ya doin'?" and finally "Hey, Timmer, how ya been?" We will just have to remember him and know he is still with us. He was the very best of all of us.

All that I have done in my career since—conducting 118 campaigns and raising over $400 million—would never have happened without Dan, Tom, Tim, and John. I always will feel a deep personal bond for and with these wonderful men. I think of each of them every day. This second book is presented as a salute to these fine, unique men. Thank you, Dan, Tom, Tim, and John, for your love and friendship.

In 2018, we will be celebrating the 350th anniversary of the founding of the French settlement known as Sault Sainte Marie. The mayor of our town is Tony Bosbous, the longest-elected mayor in the Sault's history. Tony was very instrumental in my first memoir as he wrote the foreword to the book. He helped a great deal as we dedicated the book's proceeds to the Soo Theatre Project. The work the theater group is doing for the cultural arts throughout the Sault and region and the energy and spirit they are bringing to the city are a gift to us all who love the Sault. Tony has agreed once again to write the foreword for the second book. My hope is, he remains mayor throughout the 350th anniversary of the town and we continue to have an impact and assist once again the theater. Thanks, Tony, for your continued leadership.

Colleen Arbic and her committed team at the Soo Theatre are getting the job done. They are fulfilling the dreams of many people, young and old, interested in the cultural arts. Thank you, Colleen, and your volunteers of the theater. There is no force stronger in a community than volunteers, and your group is proving it.

I want to thank once again my sisters, Mary and Kathleen, for their editing and advice. They also shared two chapters of their lives in this memoir. Thanks again, girls. Our mother, Frances, will never be dead as long as you both are still here. I love you both. Without my wife, Judy, here with me, supporting this second venture, it would have been too difficult to finish. Thanks, love; you're great. And many thanks for your lovely book-cover picture of our lighthouse in the Pines. Thanks again to Pete Campbell and Paul Byron for their delightful stories. I hope everyone enjoys their subtle humor and sees the love of where they grew up. I'm very proud to call them my friends. And thanks to my dear ole friend and former business partner Dave Rieger and his lovely wife, Myra, and my current business partners, Susan Blansett and Colleen Nelson. Thank you, everyone, for your words of encouragement and support.

To my lovely granddaughter, Isabella, all this probably never would have taken place without our school interview and class project four years ago. Thanks, sweetheart. My nephew, Brian Balmes, too was helpful early on and reviewed several drafts. My niece Shannon Schroeder was so helpful with her critique. Thanks, dear. Also, thank you to my sweet niece Bridget, whom I've always called Babe. She has always believed in her uncle and loved listening to all the family stories.

I would be very remiss if I didn't acknowledge my high school chum Rye Muir for reintroducing me to Jimmy McCarthy's beautiful poem and song "One Bright Blue Rose." Thanks again, Rye, for this very special piece. I hope you enjoy how I have used it.

And a special thanks to my family; my parents; my brothers, John and Tim; and my sisters, Mary and Kathleen. Thanks also to my Irish family, Marie and Nat from the Glen of Aherlow, and the entire O'Connor family from Tipperary; also Michael and Mary Eustace from Milltown Malbay in County Clare, Ireland; my children and their spouses: Cormac and Heather, Brendan, and Mary Frances and Andrew. To my grandchildren, Isabella, Ava, and Julia (the McCarthy girls) and Declan and Azarah (the Bigoney bunch)—my love and thanks. Our little guy who is getting bigger and bigger—our grandson, Nic Patti—has provided humor, and his lovely, lighthearted presence made writing easier and fun. I would be very remiss not to mention the support of my stepchildren and their spouses: Greg Patti and Havva, Chris Patti and Meghan, and Mary Jo Patti. Thanks, everyone, for making me proud of you each and every day. I love you all. I would be very neglectful without mentioning my McDonald family; they have always been there for me, and I love them all. Doine and Dongol and Joannie, Danny, Ruthie, and Marilyn—I know you all are enjoying this. I love you all.

Once again, Bernie Arbic of Chippewa County Historical Society (CCHS) has been a stalwart for his advice and photography gathering. Thank you so much, Bernie. Finally, I want to thank David Mallett. His poetry and music really resonate with me. Having Liam Clancy perform his rendition of "I Knew This Place" truly inspired me to write this memoir. David is a remarkable talent.

And really, finally, I want to give special thanks to those who have taken the time to read this nostalgic review and memoir. Yeats called them our beautiful memories, those sweet, precious memories, and they are that, but really more than that for me. They are a real special piece of who I am. I hope *The Sounds and Smells of My Childhood* both parts I and II have stirred your memory of your own youth wherever you were born and raised. I was part of the Soo's old times, I guess, and I remember those times as if they just happened yesterday. They were happy times. The historical significance of the town, the creative genius and resilience of its people, and the broad, majestic beauty of the St. Mary's River all are deeply implanted in my mind and in my soul. Although my life today is in Colorado, I have kept and cherished my memories of the Soo.

Like the proud, old, beautiful woman that she is, I think of her every day,

Her name I will always honor folks, I'm glad I passed her way.

A Salute to Dan Dorrity

Oh Danny boy, the pipes, the pipes are calling
From glen to glen, and down the mountain side
The summer's gone, and all the roses falling
It's you, it's you must go and I must bide.

But come ye back when summer's in the meadow
Or when the valley's hushed and white with snow
It's I'll be here in sunshine or in shadow
Oh Danny boy, oh Danny boy, I love you so.

But when ye come, and all the flow'rs are dying
If I am dead, as dead I well may be
You'll come and find the place where I am lying
And kneel and say an ave there for me.

And I shall hear, though soft you tread above me
And all my grave will warmer, sweeter be
For you will bend and tell me that you love me
And I shall sleep in peace until you come to me.

(Frederick Weatherly, "Danny Boy" [England: 1913])

A Salute to Tom Suddes

Cheer, cheer for old Notre Dame,
Wake up the echoes cheering her name,
Send a volley cheer on high,
Shake down the thunder from the sky.
What though the odds be great or small
Old Notre Dame will win over all,
While her loyal sons are marching
Onward to victory.

(Michael and John O'Shea, "Notre Dame Victory March"
[Notre Dame University Library: 1906])

A Salute to Tim Kinney

Chorus:

When Irish Eyes Are Smiling, sure 'tis like a morn in spring.
In the lilt of Irish laughter, you can hear the angels sing.
When Irish hearts are happy, all the world seems bright and gay,
And When Irish Eyes Are Smiling, sure, they steal your heart away.

Verse 1:

There's a tear in your eye and I'm wondering why,
For it never should be there at all.
With such power in your smile, sure a stone you'd beguile,
So there's never a teardrop should fall,

When your sweet lilting laughter's like some fairy song
And your eyes twinkle bright as can be.
You should laugh all the while and all other times smile,
And now smile a smile for me.

(Chorus)

(Ernest Ball and George Graff Jr., "When Irish Eyes Are Smiling" in

The Isle O' Dreams [1912])

A Salute to John McCarthy

Of all the money that e'er I spent,
I've spent it in good company.
And all the harm that e'er I've done,
Alas it was to none but me.
And all I've done for want of wit,
To memory now I can't recall,
So fill to me the parting glass,
Good bye and joy be with you all.

(Ed Sheeran, "The Parting Glass" [Warner/Chappell Music
Inc., Kobalt Music Publishing Ltd., Universal Music
Publishing Group])

Remembrance of the Soo

But sometimes on December nights,
When the air is cold,
And the Wind is right,
There's a Melody that passes through the Town.
The day is done. The lights are low,
The wheels of life are turning slow
And as these visions turn and go,
I lay me down to sleep.
Yes, I Knew This Place,
And I Knew it Well,
Every Sound,
And Every Smell

(David Mallett, "Ballad of St. Anne's Reel")

1.   Iroquois Lighthouse Original Painting, by Judy Patti

2.   Mayor Anthony Bosbous, at 5, in 1st grade, Bosbous Family Collection.

3. Myself, Colleen Arbic, and Mayor Bosbous at booksigning, photo taken by Judy Patti.

4. Pop, and Ma holding Myself, my brother John and sister Mary, McCarthy Collection.

**5.   The Cousins, Ruthie, Johnnie, Danny, and Mary, and
the baby, Myself, McCarthy Collection.**

**6.   Painting of Pop's Swing, Original painting
by Mary McCarthy.**

7. Pop (John), Ma (Julia) McCarthy with Dad (John) and his sister Doine (Geraldine), McCarthy Collection.

8. Grampa Hassett, Postmaster of Tone, Irish Fenian, Great Grandfather, McCarthy Collection.

9.   Ivan C Kincheloe, Capt, US Air Force, Kincheloe AFB named in his honor, US Air Force, Dept of Defense.

10.   KAFB entrance off Tone Road, Dept. of Defense.

11. I-500 Snowmobile Race, Walter Materna Coll, CCHS

12. Christmas Tinsel Tree, on Ashmun Street. Materna Collection, CCHS

13. Terry Sawchuck, 1955, Red Wing Goalie, Soo Evening News, provided thru Chippewa County Historical Society.

14. News Ad for the Detroit Red Wings upcoming game at the Pullar, Soo Evening News, Provided thru CCHS.

15. Fred Benoit, Boo, great friend, in 8th grade,
McCarthy Collection.

16. Jim Fuerstnau, Friz, boyhood friends, 8th grade,
McCarthy Collection.

**17. Wedding of Fred and Linda Benoit, Benoit
Family Collection.**

**18. Fred and Linda today, Golf Club owners in the Sault,
Benoit Family Collection.**

19. Roy and Gloria Dennis wedding day, neighbors on Cedar Street. Photo provided by Susan Dennis.

20. Roy Dennis, great family friend and neighbor on Cedar St. Photo provided By Susan Dennis.

21. The Dennis Family, with their baby son Michael.

22. Mom's Graduation picture, 1941, Loretto Academy.

23. Dad's Graduation Picture, 1939, Pickford High School, McCarthy Collection.

24. Wedding picture Mom & Dad, February 24, 1944, McCarthy Collection.

**25. Loretto Girls Basketball team 1941,
McCarthy Collection.**

**26. Pickford Boys basketball team, 1939,
McCarthy Collection.**

27. Sister Deborah Arment (Mother St Thomas More), IBVM, Sisters of Loretto Collection.

28. Mother St Thomas More, Music teacher, IBVM, Sisters of Loretto Collection.

29. First House on 810 Cedar Street. Family Collection

30. My Hassett cousin, Pat Wieneke. Wieneke Archives, Mike Wieneke

31. St Mary's Elementary School, Catholic Primary School. Materna Collection, CCHS.

32. Jefferson Elementary Public School, my first school. Materna Collection, CCHS.

33. Mary in 4th grade at St Mary's, 1956, McCarthy Colloection.

34. The girls, great friends Barbara Hallesy Wirt, and Mary, McCarthy Collection.

35. My sister Mary, McCarthy Collection.

36. My dear driend Rev. Peter Campbell, Peter Campbell Collection.

37. Pete with his bike, 8 yrs old, Peter Campbell Collection.

38. Pete holding the Hockey Trophy, Peter Campbell Collection.

39. Pete and his lovely wife Julie, McCarthy Collection.

**40. Boyhood friend, Paul Byron, contributor to the book,
Byron Collection.**

41. Paul Byron today at his 50th reunion.

42. Enjoying Sherman Park, summertime.

43. Watching the ships at Sherman Park.

44. Our little animal park at Sherman. Materna Collection, CCHS

**45. Callaghan's Grocery Store, Walter Materna Collection,
Chippewa County Historical Society, Sault Sainte
Marie, Michigan.**

**46. Neighborhood store, DeMolen's in the East End, on
Portage Ave, Walter Materna Coll, CCHS**

47. Bagnall's grocery store, on the Island, Walter
Materna Coll, CCHS.

48. The France grocery store, on Portage and Riverside,
Walter Materna Coll, CCHS.

49. Dalimonte's Store on Ashmun, Walter Materna
Collection, CCHS.

50. Dongol and Doines Wedding Day, My Uncle Donald,
and Aunt Geraldine, Taken from McDonald Collection.

**51. Uncle Dongol (Donald McDonald) as a young
boy in his traditional Scottish garb, Taken from
McDonald Collection.**

**52. My brother Johnnie and cousin Danny as little tots,
McDonald Collection.**

53. My dear friend Tim Kinney, in 5th grade, Tim Kinney Collection.

54. My Hassett cousin, Mike Wieneke.

55. The Famous Ritchie Auditorium, in the old Soo High School, Walter Materna Coll, CCHS.

56. Mr and Mrs Felix (Buttsy) Tavern, the great community cheerleader, Bosbous Collection

57. The Lighthouse at Bay Mills, Iroquois Point.

58. St Mary's Catholic Church in the river fog, Walter Materna Coll, CCHS.

59. St Isaac Jocques Catholic Church, East End, on Marquette Ave, Materna Coll, CCHS

60. Old St Joseph's Church, in the Southside, St Joseph Archives, CCHS.

61. Clyde's Drive In, McCarthy Collection.

**62. Sugar Island Ferryboat in the Fog
Materna Coll, CCHS.**

63. Ma wedding day, August 15, 1915, Julia Hassett, My Irish grandmother, McCarthy Collection.

64. Pop wedding day, August 15, 1915, My Irish Grandfather John McCarthy, McCarthy Collection.

65. The "Black Smoke" coming from our Carbide Plant, Materna Coll, CCHS

66. Smokestack at the Carbide, Materna Coll, CCHS.

**67. Old Moose Lodge on Ashmun, the Brown Bldg,
Walter Materna Coll, CCHS.**

**68. Painting of My Grandmother Mary Payment,
Original painting by Mary McCarthy.**

**69. Gramma and Kathy, at 706 Cedar, her first
Communion, McCarthy Collection.**

**70. The Sisters, Mary and Kathleen,
McCarthy Collection.**

71. Old Sault Savings Bank, Fassenello's Pizza, Majestic Hotel, Warners, Materna Coll, CCHS.

72. McCarthy Portable Sawmill, Grampa McCarthy, Pop, and Uncle Mike McCarthy. Taken from McCarthy Collection.

73. John's 69th birthday family picture left to right, Mary, Myself, Tim, Kathy on top, Jean and John in Spokane, WA, Photo taken by Judy Patti.

74. The McCarthy Girls, Shannon (granddaughter), Kathy (daughter), Mary Frances (granddaughter), Brenna (granddaughter), Frances (Mother & Grandmother), Mary (daughter), Bridget (granddaughter), Look at those smiles. McCarthy Collection.

**75. Mom & Dad, McCarthy Collection,
McCarthy Collection.**

76. Mike and Judy, McCarthy Collection.

**77. Myself with my grandkids Julia, next to me,
Declan with Ava, Isabella with Azarah, and Nic,
McCarthy Collection.**

**78. Our wedding picture with Judy's family, Chris, Mary
Jo, Me, Judy, and Greg, McCarthy Collection.**

79. Our McDonald Cousins, and my sisters and brothers.

80. McDonald's and McCarthy's, kids on the Farm.

81. The McCarthy Bunch at Brendan's birthday party, Myself, standing is Cormac, Brendan, My children's Mother Cynthia Card, and Mary Frances, McCarthy Collection.

82. My dearest Friend, Dr. Dan Dorrity, Photo taken by Sharon Dorrity.

83. My dearest Friend, Thomas Suddes, Photo taken by Suddes Family.

84. My dearest Friend, Tim Kinney.

85. My Beloved Brother John T. McCarthy

86. Grama and Grampa Trempe celebrating 50 years of marriage, McCarthy Collection.

87. Wedding day Mary Payment and Henry Trempe, McCarthy Collection.

88. City Hall, SSM, Old Federal Building, McCarthy Collection.

89. My Granddaughter Isabella McCarthy.

90. Dad in his Coast Guard uniform, World War II

91. Dad and Doine young kids.

92. WW I, Drum and Bugle Corps unit in the Soo.

93. The Riegers, Dave and Myra, dear friends.

94. The O'Connor Family, of Tipperary Ireland, Standing, Geraldine, Marie, Caitriona, below, Seamus, Mrs. O'Connor, and Val.

95. The Brothers, John and Myself, my favorite picture of John.

96. Christmas in Ireland, Caitriona, and Mrs O'Connor.

97. My cousin John McDonald (Danny's son) and myself.

98. Kathy as a child, with myself playing in wintertime.

99. Kathy as a baby, 1 year old.

100. My sister Kathy and her children, Conlan, Kathy, Bridget, Brenna.

101. Mother and Kathy at her wedding.

102. Dad giving away his daughter, Kathy at her wedding.

103. My dearest family friend, Marie O'Connor.

104. My daughter Mary Frances, and her husband Andrew.

105. The Old Belvedere Hotel, Materna Collection, CCHS.

106. My Granddaughter Ava McCarthy.

107. My Granddaughter Azarah Bigoney.

108. Pittsburgh Boat Supply on Portage Street, this place fed a lot of sailors, Materna Collection, CCHS.

109. My son Brendan, in the Glen of Aherlow, Ireland.

110. Old Soo High School

111. Chris and Megan Patti, Judy's son.

112. My Nephew Brian Balmes, My sister Mary's son.

113. Kathy's Husband Rich.

114. The old Carnegie Library, Walter Materna Collection, CCHS.

115. Historic Methodist Church, SSM, Materna Collection, CCHS.

116. Historic Episopal Church, SSM, Materna Collection, CCHS.

117. My son Cormac and his wife Heather, their wedding day. McCarthy Collection.

118. My Grandchildren, Declan and Azarah Bigoney.

119. The last of the Hassetts, My cousin Eva.

120. Marie and Myself deep in debate.

**121. My sister Mary, and her lovely grand-
daughter McKayla.**

122. The McCarthy's fishing, my brother John's grandkids.

123. Greg Patti and his wife Havva, Judy's son.

124. The Wedding Party, Cormac and Heather.

125. My Graduation picture from High School.

126. John and Dan at graduation with Doine and Dad.

127. My Brother John and sister in law Jean.

128. Judy and her grandson Nic, at the rink.

129. My younger sister Kathy.

130. The Kinney's, neighbors and great friends, original owners of the Antler's Bar in SSM, Walter and Lorraine, their wedding day.

131. Kresge's and Scott's department stores, Ashmun Street, SSM, Walter Materna collection, CCHS.

132. My Granddaughter Julia. McCarthy Collection.

133. My sister Mary and her family, L to R, Rob, Brian, McKayla, Ngoc, and Mary.

134. Mary Frances with her two children, Declan and Azarah.

135. The McCarthy girls, My granddaughter's, Ava, Julia, and Isabella. McCarthy Collection.

136. The Eustace's celebrating 50 years, July, Mary and Michael, my family from Miltown Malbay, in Clare, Ireland.

137. Michael and Mary's wedding day, The Eustace family, July, 1966.

138. Painting of myself, by my son Cormac, Ghourd Lake fishing trip and hike.

139. Mary Jo Patti, Judy's lovely daughter.

140. My three children as kids, Cormac, Mary Frances, and Brendan.

141. Marie O'Connor and Nat Bourke, family and dear friends at our wedding.

142. Historic Ojibway Hotel, SSM, Materna Collection, CCHS.

143. Myself and dear friend Verna Lawrence. I think of her every day.

144. My Nephew Rob Balmes, My sister Mary's son.

145. The Brothers John, Tim, and Myself on a mountain top in Ireland.

146. Our Mother celebrating her Queen for a Day, at her 75th birthday party.

147. My Cousins, the Eustace's Mary, Michael, their daughter Margaret Mary, and Myself.

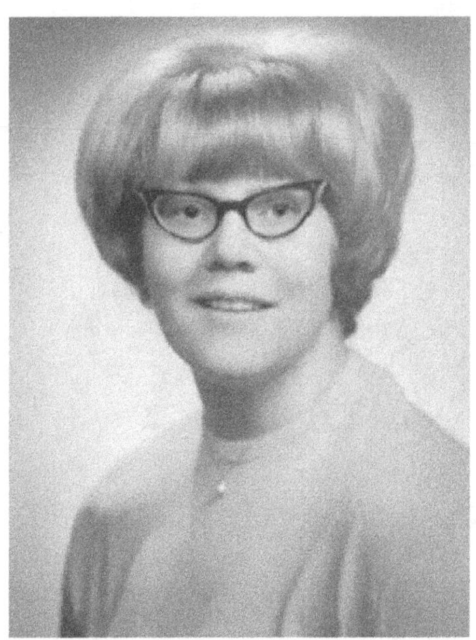

148. My beautiful cousin Ruthie McDonald, at graduation.

149. My Lovely niece Shannon, My brother John's daughter.

150. The old Soo Polyclinic. Materna Collection, CCHS.

151. My two sons, at Cheyenne Days, the Cowboys, Cormac and Brendan.

152. My younger brother Tim, his graduation.

153. Mary Frances and Andrew, on their wedding day in Jamaica.

154. The old Soo Arcade Bowling Center, on Portage Stree, SSM, Materna Collection, CCHS.

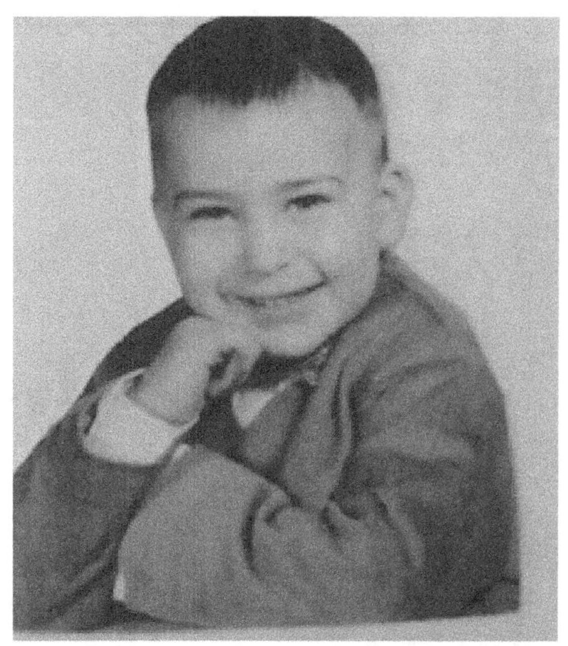

155. My brother Tim, at 2.

156. Tim and his wife Sue Ellen.

157. Tim and Sue Ellen, wedding day.

158. Old Garfield School, Spruce Street, SSM, Materna Collection, CCHS

159. Kresge Department store, luncheon Counter in the 1950's. Materna Coll. CCHS.

160. My sister Mary and cousin Ruthie McDonald, Playing at the Farm.

161. My two business partners with McCarthy-Blansett Group, at a trade show, Susan Blansett, and Colleen Nelson.

162. My brother John as a happy little boy.

163. My brother John at graduation.

164. My brothers son John.

165. John and Jean's wedding day.

166. My wife Judy in Ireland.

167. My sister Kathy's family, everyone.

168. Old Loretto Academy, my original high school.

169. My brother John, and sister Mary as kids.

170. Old McKinley School. Materna Collection, CCHS.

171. Pop, Ma, and myself.

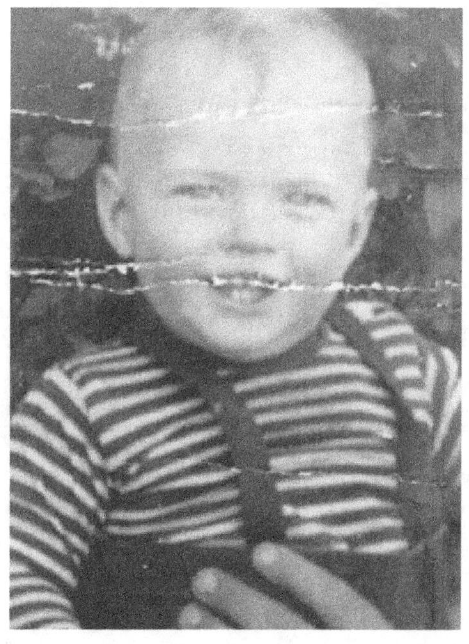

172. Myself at 1.

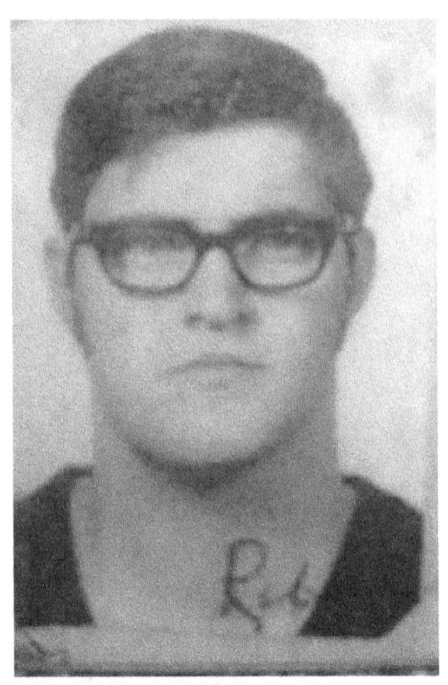

173. The day I joined the US Merchant Marine, sailed on the USS Crawford.

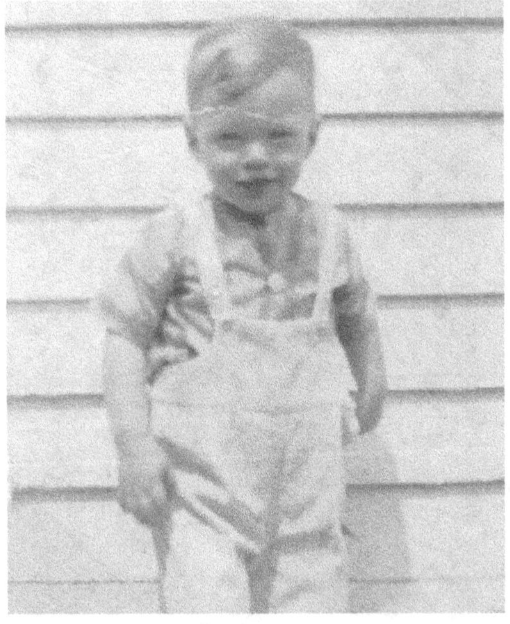

174. Myself at 3.

175. My dearly beloved brother John. RIP.

176. Our grandson Nic Patti.

177. Old Lincoln School, SSM, Materna
Collection, CCHS.

178. The Old Water Tower on Ryan and Easterday, SSM,
Materna Collection, CCHS.

179. Soo Tech basketball game held at the Pullar Stadium in the 1950's. Materna Collection, CCHS.

180. Our friends the Riegers, with myself and Judy, and Dave and Myra.

181. A & W Root Beer Stand, SSM, Materna Collection, CCHS

182. St Joseph's Catholic Elementary School, SSM, Materna Collection, CCHS.

183. St. Peter's & St Paul's Church, in South Chicago, February 24, 1944, my Parents were married here.

184. Taking My Mother and Family home to Ireland, and Miltown Malbay.

185. USS General Scott Transport Ship, my Dad's ship during WWII.

186. Wieneke Soo, Ford dealership, Ad in Soo Evening News Paper, CCHS.

187. Wieneke Soo dealership, SSM, Materna Collection, CCHS.

188. My brother John's son Michael.

**189. The line ups for a Saturday matinee at the old Soo
Theatre, Glen Gregg Collection.**

190. Myself, the Author.

Poems and Songs

Attaway, Barbara. "Let the Cat Die Down." The Collected Poems by Barbara Attaway.

Ball, Ernest, and George Graff Jr. "When Irish Eyes Are Smiling." The Isle O' Dreams. 1912.

Being an Acolyte. Taken from the Roman Catholic Missal. English translation according to the third typical edition. New Jersey: Catholic Book Publishing Corp., 2011.

Burns, Robert. "A Red, Red Rose." The Collected Poems of Robert Burns.

Coulter, Phil. "The Old Man."

Duggan, H. "The McCarthy Mill." 1904

Emerson, Ralph Waldo. "The Purpose of Life."

Fields, Eugene. "Little Boy Blue."

"Grandma." Used by permission of Derek Chandler. http://www. familyfriend-poems.com/quote/missing-grandma-quote#ixzz3qpzpCqdH.

Herrera. "Song at Benediction." Condensed article from a monograph. Complete version: smellsbells.com.

"It's Howdy Doody Time." http://www.allthelyrics.com/lyrics/ televisiontv theme lyrics kids shows soundtrack/howdy doody- lyrics-79829.html#ixzz3s-rPil1Qy J. E. Murphy. "Down at McCarthy's Party." 1882.

Kennedy, Jimmy. "Teddy Bear's Picnic." Used with permission.

Mallett, David. "I Knew This Place." BMG Ruby Songs and Reservoir Media Management Inc. All rights for BMG Ruby songs administered by BMG Rights Management (US) LLC. All rights reserved. Used by permission, reprinted by permission of Hal Leonard LLC. 50 percent control. 1978.

Mallett, David. "I Knew This Place." Reservoir Media Music and BMG Ruby Songs. All rights on behalf of Reservoir Media Music administered by Reservoir Media Management Inc. All rights reprinted and used by permission of Alfred Music. 50 percent control. 2006.

Mallett, David. "Phil Brown." BMG Ruby Songs and Reservoir Media Management Inc. All rights for BMG Ruby Songs administered by BMG Rights Management (US) LLC. All rights reserved. Used by permission, reprinted by permission of Hal Leonard LLC. 50 percent control. 1978.

Malett, David. "I Knew This Place." Resevoir Media Music and BMG Ruby Songs. All rights on behalf of Reservoir Media Music administered by Reservoir Media Management Inc. All rights reprinted and used by permission of Alfred Music. 50 percent control. 2006.

McCarthy, Jimmy. "One Bright Blue Rose."

"The Miracle of Friendship." Given to me by my mother on my eighteenth birthday.

"Notre Dame Victory March." Notre Dame University. O'Reilly, John Boyle. "Long for the Dear Old River."

"Queen of the May." A traditional Christian (Catholic) Marian hymn sung by St. Mary's Boys Choir in 1958.

Sheeran, Ed. "The Parting Glass." Warner/Chappell Music Inc., Kobalt Music Publishing Ltd., Universal Music Publishing Group.

Travis, Randy. "He Walked on Water."

Weatherly, Frederick. "Oh Danny Boy." England: 1913.

Williamson, Fred. "Flower of Scotland." National anthem of Scotland.

Yeats, W. B. "The Lake Isle of Innisfree." The Collected Poems of W. B. Yeats. 1989

Credits

Photos used in this autobiography were from the archives of the Chippewa County Historical Society and Bernie Arbic, its president. Others were taken from the Department of Defense Library, IBVM, the Sisters of Loretto collection, the Glenn Gregg collection (one of the historic photographers from the Sault similar to Walter and Carl Materna), the Bayliss Public Library, and the collections of the McDonald, McCarthy, Kinney, Dennis, Bigoney, Suddes, Wieneke, Campbell, Byron, and Lawrence families.

Permission was given to use the original painting by Judy Patti of the Iroquois Point Lighthouse in Bay Mills, Michigan.

Permission to use "I Knew This Place," words by David Mallett, copyright © 1978, BMG Ruby Songs and Reservoir Media Management Inc. All rights for BMG Ruby Songs administered by BMG Rights Management (US) LLC. All rights reserved. Used by permission, reprinted by permission of Hal Leonard LLC. 50 percent control.

"I Knew This Place," words by David Mallett, copyright © 2006, Reservoir Media Music and BMG Ruby Songs. All rights on behalf of Reservoir Media Music administered by Reservoir Media Management Inc. All rights reprinted and used by permission of Alfred Music. 50 percent control.

Index